How to Reach

the Ones You Love

BOOKS BY NYLA WITMORE

I Was an Overcommitted Christian (Tyndale 1979)

How To Reach the Ones You Love

ILLUSTRATED BY THE AUTHOR

HOW TO REACH

THE ONES YOU LOVE

HELP FOR THE FAMILY

BY NYLA WITMORE

HERE'S LIFE PUBLISHERS, INC.

San Bernardino, California 92402

HOW TO REACH THE ONES YOU LOVE
Help for the Family
By Nyla Witmore

Published by
HERE'S LIFE PUBLISHERS, INC.
P. O. Box 1576
San Bernardino, CA 92402

Library of Congress Catalogue Card 81-81849
ISBN 0-89840-016-3
HLP Product No. 950220

Manufactured in the United States of America

To my loved ones

Jerry

Michael

Christopher

My mother

My brother

My father, who has gone
to be with the Lord

TABLE OF CONTENTS

FOREWORD

In an unusually practical way, this gifted author shares from her own personal experience with a style reminiscent of Erma Bombeck and Ann Landers. She covers serious topics simply and clearly, yet couched in language that can bring laughter along with tears.

Any believer genuinely concerned about loved ones and their divine relationship—whether inside or outside the immediate family—will find invaluable helps and encouragement in these pages.

One of the great benefits of this book is firsthand lessons on how to profit from your mistakes in this very important phase of personal witnessing. You can learn from the experience of others, and this is a most pleasant and painless way to learn.

Intriguing chapter titles add to the joy of reading. "Why Do I Feel Like the Lone Ranger?", "Believers, Babies and Brides," "Calendar Conniving," "Household Plants" are typical.

The brief, pungent, incisive petitions at the end of most chapters lend a personal touch to the chapter's teachings. You will be blessed and encouraged as you read, study, then review the pages of this valuable volume.

Dennis Rainey

National Director, Family Ministry
Campus Crusade for Christ
Little Rock, Arkansas

ACKNOWLEDGMENTS

Writers must be among the most grateful people on God's earth...for without the input from life, friends and acquaintances and a sprinkling of "authorities" to give credibility and balance to our writings, our pages would be blank, bland and trite.

I am among the thankful. So, to those whose input blessed me and in turn compelled me to crank out endless reams of verbiage, I acknowledge their contributions in making this book possible.

Thanks to...

—Lyle Jacobson, Larry Taylor and Jack Mitchell: pastors,

—Jo Jacobson and Gail MacDonald: pastors' wives,

—Drs. Kaye Cook, Robert Joss, Harold Bussell and Raymond Pendleton: academicians, counselors and psychologists,

—Dr. E. John Steinhilber M.D.: psychiatrist,

—Romine Brooks, a special man of God privileged to work with the campus ministry of Here's Life,

—My husband and sons, for putting up with a couple of intense weeks...and never complaining,

—Special prayer warriors, Barbara Blankinship in particular. (Never have I felt such a propelling force of prayer in making the "right words" happen on paper!)

—For those who preferred anonymity, God bless you for sharing your stories with me.

—And, finally, to Dave Enlow, Editorial Director of Here's Life Publishers, who from the beginning of my writing career/ministry has cheered from the sidelines and challenged me to reach beyond what I ever thought possible to attain.

"I strain to reach the end of the race and receive the prize for which God is calling us up to heaven because of what Christ Jesus did for us" (Philippians 3:14 Living Bible).

INTRODUCTION

When I think of leading loved ones to Christ, I think of more than leading them to a conversion experience. I think of continuous long-term caring—a caring that keeps the doors open for a perpetual witness.

Why is it so hard to share our faith in Christ with loved ones? Often, it's because we see them every day. Or we're emotionally tied to them in some way. When they're up close, we see their "warts" and they see ours.

When you're close to people, your spiritual impact on them can be compared to a beautiful songbird outside a window. After the bird has been there for a while you don't hear its music, at least not consciously.

Likewise, our loved ones may not be conscious of our influence on them. Or, witnessing can be like a dripping faucet, irritating to people and very consciously perceived!

With loved ones you don't usually appear as a sparkling, gem-like witness. Billy Graham can be that, but you and I don't usually have that effect.

In the family context it may be more difficult to pass out gospel tracts, recommend good books, or go through a detailed salvation presentation, because our families don't always take our recommendations seriously. But because we are so close to them, we often feel compelled to persist in our witnessing until our loved ones have experienced the fullness of God.

To meet this need, plenty of books have been written that give "Ten Easy Steps To Sharing Your Faith," and so on. My book tells you what to do before you've read all the others!

If you are plagued by the "guilties" because you haven't been consistent in sharing your faith, or if you

13

lack confidence in witnessing, this book should help you turn past failures into positive learning experiences. Everybody makes mistakes. It's what you do with mistakes that counts. With the proper care, some mistakes become miracles!

Remember, no matter how many times you've failed...God can still use you!

Nyla Witmore

Section One

PURPOSE

Why Do I Feel Like the Lone Ranger?

Believers, Babies and Brides

CHAPTER 1

Why Do I Feel Like the Lone Ranger?

You've picked up this book hoping that finally you can find a way out of the prison of guilt—a prison self-imposed because you haven't been able to bring a loved one to Christ.

You may be a college student trying to witness to a roommate, or a parent trying to witness to a wayward child. You may be a husband who is trying to share Christ with an agnostic wife, or a girl trying to pray her fiance into the Kingdom.

You may be a business person wanting to help a co-worker find peace with God.

But you're frustrated. You could hang your head and mutter under your breath, "Well, I guess I'm just not cut out for this witnessing or evangelism stuff. Let somebody who has the gift do it."

Whoa! Not so fast! Although some Christians have been given the specific gift of evangelism, Scripture doesn't confine witnessing to those individuals. There is a way to do your part, however small, in helping reach others for Christ.

"Not me," you may say. Welcome to the Anxious Ambassadors Association. As an ambassador for Christ, you may have known the pain of being spiritually un-productive at times. You are plagued with doubts about your ability to communicate the gospel. You ask yourself, "Why can't she (he) see the simplicity of recognizing God's plan for mankind? It seems so clear—

to me at least."

You may decide to try some other witnessing routes:

Put Christian messages in your holiday newsletter.

Stuff Halloween snacks with gospel hand-outs.

Buy Christian bumper stickers for your car.

Wear lapel pins with Christian slogans.

Hang around local coffee shops, armed with tracts.

As you read over the list you realize that some of these gestures could be met with lukewarm acceptance. For example, if you tried some of these on your Great-uncle Willie, he might cut you out of his will permanently unless you "stop this nonsense!"

At this point, you may think a little expert coaching would help, so you join a church visitation group that calls on prospective church members. Or, you may attend a meeting designed to teach lay men and women how to share their faith. Finally, armed with verses and a partially memorized, sequential order for presentation, you think, "Now I'll finally be able to win the world for Christ."

A witnessing opportunity comes. The air is full of expectancy. Convinced the Holy Spirit is empowering you, you go through your gospel presentation. You work your main points into the conversation:

God loves you.

God wants perfection.

No one is perfect because all have sinned.

No, even as hard as you try, you'll never be good enough.

God has provided a way for you to be good enough.

That way is through Jesus.

God will see you as sinless and forgiven once you have invited Jesus into your heart as your Savior and have accepted His all-sufficient sacrifice for you.

Then you can have fellowship with God and be at peace.

Your presentation is complete. But the individual to

whom you are witnessing doesn't respond. How do you handle the reaction? How do you face what seems to be rejection of yourself and of Christ's message? Do you kick stones? Bury your sorrows in a triple-thick ice cream sundae? Get angry with God?

It is during these moments you know what it feels like to be a "Lone Ranger" for God. Your face flushes. You feel as though you've been thrust into a spotlight and you don't know what to do.

To go through all this with a complete stranger is one thing. But to endure these steps with a close friend or family member is another. More than likely, **the closer you are to the person, the greater the potential anxiety and embarrassment when witnessing.**

I wanted to share these thoughts because I, like you, have experienced those desperately frustrating times.

During my high school years I started witnessing with some success. And when dating a skeptic or an agnostic I began to argue a lot. Eventually I became persistent. I decided I would tell others of God's love whether they wanted me to or not.

By the time I graduated from college, steam-roller tactics had crept into my gospel presentation, and I found I was becoming increasingly insensitive to the viewpoints of others.

In my early married years, I had a purse crammed full of tracts and other witnessing aids. Boy, was I prepared! Funny thing, however, even though I had all the ammunition, when I attempted to introduce the gospel, I felt awkward.

I'd been married about seven years when I experienced a spiritual renewal. I had always been a go-getter by nature, and my new commitment made me even more so. My church activities intensified: making craft items for bazaars, leading Bible studies, serving on boards and committees, going to prayer meetings. Unfortunately, I was rapidly heading for a spiritual burnout.

During this time my husband, Jerry, a wonderful

church-going man, was feeling under pressure, sensing that I wanted him to have the same spiritual zeal and intensity I had.

I pushed and pulled him, and even tried to shame him into taking on more spiritual responsibility in the church and at home. I connived, rearranged his schedules, persuaded other men to ask him to do things. Secretly, I hoped he would experience a carbon copy of my spiritual renewal.

But since none of these tactics worked, you can imagine how defeated I was. Fortunately, four years later, a moment of truth came which rescued our marriage, preserved my sanity and freed Jerry to grow spiritually at his own pace.

From that experience, I learned to allow others to grow at God's pace for them—not mine. And I also learned to develop a more natural witnessing style.

Now it has occurred to me that maybe there are others who feel they are spiritually ineffective or are plagued with guilt when they think they've turned someone away from the gospel. Wouldn't it be great if I could help them find new ways of dealing with frustration and difficult witnessing situations!

I don't claim to be a miracle worker. But if anything written here can help to firm up sagging confidence, I'll feel I have been of some small benefit.

———————

Lord, I want to serve You better. Set me free to discover my strengths, to learn from my failures, to become a more effective witness for You. Amen.

CHAPTER 2

Believers, Babies and Brides

Overzealous believers, babies and brides—what a mixture! Surprisingly, they have much in common.

Consider a baby. It is ravenously hungry for attention from birth, stays close to its mother, is self-centered, wants everything "ten minutes ago," is very vocal about its own needs and unaware of the needs of others.

Not all overly zealous believers would have all those same characteristics, but perhaps enough to make my comparison valid.

Marsha, for instance, was a struggling striver from the day of her spiritual birth. She couldn't understand why others in the church didn't take spiritual growth as seriously as she did. Whenever an announcement appeared in the bulletin regarding new activities, services or learning opportunities, Marsha was on the doorstep ten minutes early with notebook and pencil in hand. Her spiritual appetite was almost insatiable.

Marsha's friend, Penny, who often came to church with her, was another new believer. Her hand was the first to be lifted to answer questions in class and the first raised as a volunteer. She was extremely vocal about her inner thoughts and her expectations for others. The brief acquaintance she had with the Bible was sufficient, she figured, to make her an outspoken authority on everything.

Penny wanted and needed to be heard, but she was insensitive to the needs of those around her. Not because she was inherently or intentionally callous—she simply hadn't learned that the same Lord who tamed her soul would eventually get around to taming her tongue, providing she cooperated. Cooperating does not come easily to babies!

Penny was caught in an immature spiritual stage. Not a great deal has been written about the growth stages of the Christian life. Often, when churches focus on getting people inside the door and saved, the spiritual pediatrics are planned in only a catch-as-catch-can way.

Church leaders sometimes feel that if you keep inviting new Christians to meetings and get them signed up on committees, their spiritual growth will come naturally. Sometimes it does; at other times the church roster is weighted with the walking wounded, those who have been "churched-to-death" or who are "zealoused-out."

This chapter hopefully explains the growth process in such a way that you will find yourself less critical of the seemingly overzealous in your midst. And should you be on the list of those forceful busy-bees, maybe this chapter will help you see yourself as you really are. Maybe you won't be quite so hard on yourself, or others. By understanding this now, the remaining chapters should take on clearer meaning.

There have been a few periods in my life in which I was overzealous spiritually. I've always attributed them to my naturally enthusiastic personality. But in my case, such times of zealousness came following one of these events: (1) a spiritual experience that provided me with profound insight, (2) frustration with myself or (3) frustration with others.

What makes you overzealous spiritually? A cause? An injustice? A campaign? If you are stirred in a public situation, are you different in private? What makes you fervent when you're with loved ones? What is it that turns quiet evenings into verbal scrimmages about spiritual things? Look carefully—maybe you can detect a pattern.

Like Marsha and Penny, a lot of us who are in spiritual infancy have a tendency to overdo with activities. "If one Bible study is great, two or three will be even better," we reason. That works for a while because new Christians and renewed believers have tremendous stamina accompanied by strong spiritual appetites.

This voracious appetite is good—at first. Those early days are important for developing friendships and fellowship bonds. Spiritual infants need close and frequent contacts just as babies do physically.

Did you know that when a baby first comes into the world, it can't differentiate between itself and its mother? In some strange mystical way, it assumes it is one with her. Not until several months later do the tears begin when Mama leaves the room. Why? Because baby now perceives that part of himself has just left him and he's lonely. Even when mother assures him, "Mommy will be back soon," baby can't fathom the meaning.

There is pain associated with separation of baby and mother just as there is with a spiritual baby and God. He promises, "I will never leave you nor forsake you...Lo, I will be with you always..." but the new Christian has trouble internalizing those words of comfort. By nature, we humans want visible, tangible proof for everything. Living on faith is not our idea of the easy life.

Growth, however, must come. Real babies, after they have learned to crawl, begin to experiment with walking upright. At first a mother, father or sibling will hold out fingers for tiny hands to grasp. It isn't long before one finger lets loose and then another. Mother is nearby and is fighting the urge to rush over and kiss away the first tears when the baby falls.

Though it is hard to restrain herself, she knows that persistent intervention at the first moment of trauma or trouble will hinder more than help her child. Why? The child will become more dependent on Mother and less self-reliant. A baby can't develop balance and leg strength if Mother's helping fingers are always touching.

Let's compare that with the spiritual life. God wants us to develop balance and strong spiritual legs. He stands back, ready to rush in if we're in trouble. He's never more than a prayer away.

The first time a believer notices that God seems to have backed away slightly, he doesn't know what it means. Those first few weeks when God's presence is so tangible, when the glow is inside and out, are the times he can rely totally on Him without taking much personal responsibility. Then things change. Eventually Marsha and Penny will have to face this too.

At one time, I thought I was losing my faith—I had reached the toddler stage. I began to question my renewal experience, thinking maybe it had been simply an emotional episode. I used to feel so close to God. Why wasn't the feeling as strong now?

Most people, when they approach this toddler stage, consider three posibilities: (1) I'll stick it out—maybe things will get better. (2) Maybe, if I increase the pace and try to recapture the experiences that were so satisfying in the earlier stages, I'll make it. Or (3) What's the use, maybe I'm not cut out for this "Christian living stuff."

Let me comment on the second choice—trying to recapture the earlier satisfying experiences. Some of us begin to covet certain experiences that will restore the joy of our salvation and we begin to look each week for a "can you top this" moving of the Holy Spirit. A toddler-stage Christian can become overly zealous in pursuit of reviving old memories.

The toddler stage has another characteristic that contributes to overzealousness. It's the belief in a personal omnipotence: "I can do anything. I can't burn out—I'm a super-Christian!" Little children express this when they defy danger by climbing into the cupboards and apple trees and onto the neighbor's electric fence! Christians do it when they unrealistically assess their gifts and stamina and their ability to perform spiritually.

The same unrealistic assessment of limits pops up

again during adolescent stages of Christian growth. For example, a renewed believer thinks, "I can be on the church council, lead the evangelism training program, attend the men's fellowship breakfast twice a month, teach a midweek and Sunday morning Bible study, plus sing in the choir—all without burning out." Adolescent Christians don't pick and choose acitvities very well.

Sometimes an outside event will trigger over-zealousness. For example, if a believer loses a loved one through death, he may respond with adrenalin-pumping intensity. "I should be doing something to rid the world of all this pain and sin!" he says to himself. Soon the quest to save another loved one shows up with white-knuckled fervor, and the crusade is on.

Some zealousness is good, even necessary. But un-checked, it can become harmful.

God has provided a check-and-balance system for overzealousness: the fellowship of believers. Other believers are there to tell us, "You're doing too much...you're pushing too hard. Take a rest."

My first reaction to fellow Christians who tried to slow me down was, "They're trying to weaken my com-mitment to Christ." But actually they were trying to help me conserve my strength so I wouldn't run the first few laps with finish-line intensity.

It's important, too, to make sure new believers don't form their own clique. They need seasoned mentors and guides sprinkled among them. Otherwise, they merely reinforce each other's immature zeal.

It's good to assess, from time to time, where we are on the spiritual continuum. Where are you on the growth line? Are you an infant? Toddler? Adolescent? Or have you reached a mark of adulthood and maturity?

Hopefully, this will help you view yourself and others with a more understanding, merciful eye.

Now, let's look at brides. What do they have in common with new and renewed believers? Listen to the following bride:

"Oh, you can't believe how wonderful it is to be married! It's **fan-tas-tic!** I don't know how I ever lived without Russell! He makes me feel so, so complete—so needed—so loved! **Everyone** ought to get married, at least once!"

Some new believers do the same thing with their relationship with Jesus. I know I did:

"Jesus is my whole life. I can't get enough of Him. He's made my life meaningful and given me a true purpose and fulfillment. If there were some way I could get the whole world to take a 'Jesus Pill,' I'd do it."

Symptoms of a new or renewed love are beautiful. There's something to be said for the blushing, gushing bride and the glow-to-the-toe believer:

1. There is great intensity in focusing all energies on the relationship at hand.

2. There's a lack of self-consciousness in proclaiming that love.

3. Bystanders, warmed and reminded of their own blissful experiences, muse, "Ah, to be like that again."

On the flip side, there can be other reactions. Some onlookers might say, "Don't tell me I acted like **that** when I was newly married!" Or, "How embarrassing...all that hugging in public." Or, "Just wait a few years, then they'll have a good **dose of realism** and their feet will touch ground again." Don't people sometimes say the same things about new Christians?

Maybe this is why onlookers are so critical of zealous believers. It is a relative judgment made by people who consider themselves to be the norm. One man describes a new believer as enthusiastic, while another says of the same man, "He's a fanatic." It all depends on where you're standing.

An atheist may think the man who attends church regularly is a fanatic. The warm-the-pew-on-Sundays-only person is critical of the one who gets deeply involved in church activities during the week. On and on it goes, with each person looking askance at the one who is busier or more involved.

It seems that no matter what excesses we observe, new and renewed believers are among the most effective witnesses. They draw others by their enthusiasm and changed lives. Perhaps they can be forgiven if they alienate those who would have been offended anyway at the mere whisper of the name of Jesus. While excesses in speech or actions cannot be justified, I can forgive the gushing bride-like believer and trust that maturity will win in the end.

———————

Father, I need to understand my Christian life as a long process. Help me grow through the necessary ages and stages with grace and dignity. Give me gentleness in helping others grow through their stages too. Amen.

Section Two

CHRISTIAN ON THE OFFENSIVE—OR AN OFFENSIVE CHRISTIAN?

CHAPTER 3

Calendar Conniving

Situation A: Mary lay in bed, staring at the acoustical tile patterns over her bed. Her mind didn't register any of the shapes or configurations above her because she was too busy working out some mental configurations of her own. How to get Bob (a regular date for the last four months) to go to church with her...that was foremost in her mind.

"Let's see, I could tell him we've been invited to the Barkers for dinner following the services. He knows Dottie Barker is a fantastic cook. Yes, that's what I'll do. It shouldn't be too hard to arrange."

Situation B: Mark hadn't meant to fall in love with Cindy. He knew his parents would be upset if they knew he was getting really serious about a girl whose faith was different. All along he had told himself they would remain just friends with no serious attachments. It didn't work out that way. Now he was hooked.

He tried to break off the relationship, but Cindy had cried and, oh, how he hated to see anyone that lovely cry!

One night he decided to tell her of his predicament. He chose a nice, quiet, out-of-the-way Italian restaurant not far from campus. After dinner the waitress brought coffee and the two held hands as they sipped espresso.

"Cindy, I've been meaning to tell you something for a long time. I figure I owe you the truth about why I tried to break up with you."

Cindy listened intently, her hand stiffening as Mark spoke.

"My parents are the happiest married people I know. One of the biggest reasons for the success of their marriage is that they both believe in God."

"So...I believe in God too." She bent her head.

"But it's different, Cindy. The God my parents and I believe in incorporates the person of Jesus. Your religion doesn't."

"Oh, Mark. Don't be archaic. We're all headed in the same direction...we just go about it differently. You know the saying, 'All roads lead to Rome.'"

"I don't believe that. And that's what makes us different. I can't imagine spending the rest of my life with someone and all the while knowing that when I die I'll go to heaven but she wouldn't be able to join me. I really want to ask you to be my wife...but...I love you too much to be satisfied with having our oneness be only physical. I want spiritual oneness too."

Cindy looked up, her eyes brimming with tears.

"I had no idea it was that important to you, Mark. I can't promise to change but I'll try. I'll really try to see if this Jesus is all you say He is."

Cindy began classes with Mark's campus pastor. She went alone. Mark had said he wanted it that way, so she'd feel free to ask the real questions in her heart. Otherwise, he feared she might hold back to please him. Their future was at stake.

Cindy had lots of questions. Twelve weeks' worth—that's how long she had agreed to meet with the pastor. There was so much to learn.

During the seventh meeting the pastor spoke about the nature and purpose of Christ. In earlier sessions Cindy had learned about the nature of God, a teaching which was fairly easy to blend with her "father-figure" concept of God. Recognizing Jesus as the Christ was going to be much more difficult for her.

First the pastor led her to the Old Testament prophecies and then to the proof texts found in the New Testament. Before this, she had heard these things only in Christmas carols and had never made a biblical connection. Suddenly, illumination came. She realized she had questioned His deity before but now she was personally confronted with Christ Himself. There was no longer any doubt. She was convinced that Jesus was the Son of God. There could be no other answer to all those fulfilled prophecies. (You can imagine the fellowship that evening between Cindy and Mark!)

Think about the two examples I've just presented. Mary's manipulation was subversive. Mark's was direct. Which produced potentially longer lasting results?

Have you ever been guilty of trying to arrange the calendar in order to trap someone into a confrontation with the gospel? Something inside me cringes at justifying furtive means to a good or noble end. Perhaps it's because I've seen firsthand the poison and paralysis that come to a relationship from going behind someone's back. Even if the other person never finds out, guilt grows.

Sometimes the ones we're trying to catch for the Lord catch on to our games. I've heard parents connive to arrange for one person's child to be asked by another's child to come to a youth rally. (You'd better believe the kids can tell a put-up job when they see one. They're experts at recognizing real or counterfeit concern.)

Another example of manipulation is when a wife will arrange to have another man invite her bashful husband to a men's church club breakfast. Sometimes it works— if it's genuine. But if the one fingered to do the asking is not truthfully gregarious, the unsuspecting husband becomes very suspecting. It is better to pray persistently that the Lord will do the selecting and will nudge the right man for the job.

When you're doing the inviting, it is important to keep the invitation natural. If the name of someone to invite to something pops into your mind, follow the lead and test the waters. Pray ahead of time for open doors, and if the situation develops easily, you'll know you were the right person. Through prayer, bind Satan to keep him from interfering, and you needn't worry if your invitation is turned down. Just know it was not in God's timing. **God is never late!**

Inside me is an imaginary box tied with a "faith" bow. On the box it says, **God can do anything He wants to, with anyone He wants to, where He wants to, when He wants to.** When I come to a roadblock in my evangelistic travels, I mentally clap my hands and I whisper, "Okay, God, You've got something else in mind. I can hardly wait to find out what it is." Then if I'm really observant and praise Him for the detours, I often recognize another opportunity or lesson.

For example, I was on a Christian talk show not long ago. It was my first. I was excited as I sat in the holding room. The first guest went on. He was a r-e-a-l s-l-o-w t-a-l-k-e-r. The show moved along and finally, with only a half hour left, I began to wonder if I would ever get on. I had a message of encouragement to share on how not to become a burned-out Christian. I was certain the world needed to hear my nuggets of wisdom.

As the clock ticked down to the last 10 minutes, I thought, **God, You made a mistake.** That interviewer just wasn't being led by the Spirit if he let the first guest talk for the full two hours.

Soon the associate producer came in with her clipboard. When she asked, "Do you think you could stay over for tomorrow?" I sighed with relief. Maybe God did still intend for me to share.

Well, that roadblock was no accident. It was the best thing that could have happened.

The next morning came, and by then I felt like an old hand at the business of preparing for talk shows. I prayed, "God, I trusted You yesterday; I trust You today. You must know something I don't, and I'm going to give You the benefit of the doubt."

Again, I sat with the other guests in the holding room. One hour went by. Another half hour and there were still two of us left. The other guest was a famous author so I figured this was strike two. But by now my faith was really growing and I was fully trusting. I knew God could see this circumstance from beginning to end, though I could only see through the knothole of the fence where I was standing. So I trusted God for the best and, realizing the world didn't have to hold its breath waiting for me to speak, I accepted what seemed inevitable with a submissive will.

The next thing I knew, with only 30 minutes left and a celebrity there who just "happened to drop by" to surprise the show host, the other guest and I were pushed through the doors and onto the stage.

In the last 10 minutes of the program, I not only was able to share 80% of what was in my book, **I Was an Overcommitted Christian,** but as the cameraman signaled "one minute," a Bible verse popped into my mind to tie my whole message together. And God gave me such peace and relaxation that I never stammered once.

But the best part came later when I spoke with a friend who had tuned in the program that day to watch **me** (she thought!). However, she had a problem that was similar to that of the woman who was the show's first guest, and as my friend watched that woman, she was filled with hope and faith that God could take care of her own problem!

Don't be afraid to let God arrange and rearrange your witnessing opportunities.

Don't be surprised if you start with the intent to witness or share God's love with someone and you find God has chosen to use someone else just then. Yield to it. Don't fight for "your time." It's not your time; it's God's.

CHAPTER 4

Jesus Wallpaper: How Much Is Too Much?

Symbols are a normal part of living. "John loves Mary" carved into an old oak tree, an engagement ring, a T-shirt with a school crest or insignia, an American flag, and for a Christian, an open Bible on the coffee table or a cross worn about the neck. These are but a few of the symbols of love and loyalty common to our culture.

When I was a new Christian, I loved crosses. That symbol held great meaning for me. In fact, I remember scouring the display cases in jewelry stores whenever we went on a vacation. There was always one more cross to add to my collection. Once I had six or seven, enough for nearly every day of the week.

Then came the lapel pins and the buttons with Christian slogans. I didn't think I was gaudy, but maybe others thought so. I loved Jesus so much I didn't care who knew it. In fact, I hoped strangers would approach me to ask about my adornments.

It was the same at home. I loved posters and plaques bearing Scripture selections or words of inspiration. My collection rivaled my boys' assortments of football pennants.

Was that wrong? Of course not, but the Bible has some helpful suggestions. While on the one hand Old Testament Jews were to keep religious articles "as frontlets between the eyes" (reminders if you will), the New Testament message addresses the issue of excesses.

The apostle Paul tells us, "Let your moderation be known unto all" (Philippians 4:5, KJV). Later, in 1 Timothy 2:9, he speaks of adorning ourselves in modest apparel.

What is moderation? The dictionary reveals: "within reasonable limits; not excessive or extreme."

How can you discern how much is enough? One pastor I know asks the question, "To what extent do your religious observances cause inconvenience to others?"

In recent years I have become quite intent in seeking the answer for myself. I periodically ask my husband and children, "Do you sense I am being inconsiderate? Do I seem to be doing too much in one area?" (It might not be a bad idea to consider asking that question of my friends and peers occasionally.) Another way of phrasing that question is, "Do you feel pushed out of my life when I am involved in other things?"

I've been asking friends and acquaintances whom I admire, "How do you keep balance and moderation and still accomplish all God has in mind for you?"

One woman said, "I have my devotions and Bible study when the children are napping or in school. I try never to take time away from my husband to complete my study."

One friend tells me she would rather I call her during the day to chat because she likes to keep evenings free for her husband and children. I admire her for telling me her preference.

When I first suggested that to someone myself, I was embarrassed. I thought, what if that person needs a sympathetic ear at 8 p.m.? Wouldn't I be refusing to give a cup of water to someone in need?

Then I discovered my friends were not offended by my suggestion. It forced both of us to weigh the importance of our conversation with a more judicial and economizing eye. The easy habit of picking up the phone in the evening was becoming more disciplined. Furthermore, one friend told me her husband had been fidgety over our long evening conversations and was happy to see us deliberately curtail our dialogue. Being considerate and practical paid off.

I know someone might say, "She's shirking her responsibility for Christian witnessing." Hold it! I'm not talking about keeping a lock on your phone or mouth, or hiding every shred of evidence of your Christian faith.

Think about Christ's example for a moment. There were times when He was not available to the masses. Sometimes He needed rest. Other times He determined it was not appropriate to minister. In fact, in the Sermon on the Mount He gave clear instructions for the most effective ways to share spiritual truths with others.

In one passage He speaks of sharing without criticizing. "Don't criticize, and then you won't be criticized. For others will treat you as you treat them. And why worry about a speck in the eye of a brother when you have a board in your own? Should you say, 'Friend, let me help you get that speck out of your eye,' when you can't even see because of the board in your own? Hypocrite! First get rid of the board. Then you can see to help your brother" (Matthew 7:1-5, TLB).

Here's the application: If posters, religious music or literature, crosses, etc., are blatantly used to point out the sins of others close to us, our motives may be wrong. Why? Because nine times out of ten we have been so busy looking at their blemishes, we couldn't see the boil festering between our own two eyes.

This lesson was brought home to me in an incident a fews years ago involving my oldest son, then age 11.

My two young sons were engaging in the usual sibling rivalry. "What are these God-fearing, church-going boys of mine doing?" I shouted. "They're killing each other, that's what they're doing!"

That evening, Jerry read a proverb from **The Living Bible.** I gloated, thinking how appropriate it was for the boys in light of the earlier donnybrook and verbal accusations.

Later, after the children went to bed, I got out a large piece of paper and proceeded to write the proverb again in bold black letters. Then I placed the poster on the refrigerator door as a reminder. It read:

"Don't testify spitefully against an innocent neighbor. Why lie about him? Don't say, 'Now I can pay him back for all his meanness to me!'"

Morning came. The boys hastily ate their cereal, grabbed lunch money and dashed out the door. Just before 3 p.m. they came bounding through the front door. Mike, one of my sons, had brought a friend with him.

It wasn't long before the friend said, "What is **that** on your refrigerator?"

Mike turned red, embarrassment blazoned across his face. Quickly, he changed the subject and hurried his friend to another part of the house.

When the friend had gone home, Mike came into the kitchen. He snatched the billboard from the refrigerator door. "Don't do that to me, Mother. You don't have to broadcast my problem to the whole world."

What did I learn from that? First, **don't put up signs for anybody's benefit but your own.** Second, **keep spiritual lessons between those directly involved. No billboarding of sins for outsiders to view.** Third, **before you put up signs, ask yourself, "Who will this help? Who will it hurt?"**

I could easily have defended my point or my right to express myself. I also could have alienated a young boy whom Jesus wanted to reach in a gentler way.

My friend Mary has a loving touch with furnishings. Acquaintances and visitors regularly comment to her, "There's something different about your home."

That something different goes beyond her gift of hospitality and warmth. It's the touch of Christian love and caring that gives each room a sweet and calming atmosphere.

Mary's Christian lifestyle is reflected in her treatment of others. It shows when she's shopping, marketing, or meeting strangers for the first time. Mary is genuine.

I would dare say, her Christian witness would radiate even if her home were devoid of crosses, Bibles or posters. Her life makes me ask myself, "Could others tell I'm a Christian if I didn't wear a cross?"

I know of another woman whose home by comparison appears gaudy with sacred bric-a-brac and religious mementos. Nothing in the home speaks of the interests of her husband. Some posters have been up for six or seven years. Door knockers, stickers on door knobs, even plaques in the bathroom refer in some way to her faith.

With "Jesus wallpaper" everywhere, her husband can barely find a place to hang his fishing trophies. After visiting her home one day, I took a fresh look at the things I had scattered throughout my own house. Six years from now, will mine look like hers?

I took the matter up with God during one of my private prayer times. I had to ask, "Have I become attached to **things,** even though they are spiritual and religious **things?**"

There was only one way to find out. I began to remove the excess clutter. I had no idea it would be so hard. At first I felt I was denying my faith by deleting posters and stripping certain walls. It reminded me of a feeling I had when I was a little girl. I was afraid to miss church or Sunday school for fear something bad might happen to me. Now I felt somewhat the same way, and I wondered why.

I had never before thought of "idolatry" in connection with the posters, but now I did. The posters, in and of themselves, were all right—my use of them was wrong.

I learned some things from that soul-rending exercise.

I must regularly rearrange my surroundings to prove to myself that I am not too attached to material things. I find it helpful and aesthetic to rotate posters and plaques seasonally, so I won't become numbed and oblivious to the messages written on them. I need to ask other members of the family for their input in wall displays and arrangements. It doesn't hurt to ask, "Do you think this is a bit much?"

Finally, I'm learning to assure my family the Bible verses over the sink are for my benefit, not theirs. If I need to memorize one for a class assignment, I try to monitor the number of days it has been sitting there. After a couple of weeks, it's time for it to come down.

If you come to my home now, you will see a number of translations of the Bible on the bookshelves. On occasion you may see a poster on the side wall of the refrigerator...Jerry likes the front of the refrigerator clean and clear. And you will see a modest plaque over the kitchen sink window. It reads:

Bless Our Home

Father, that we cherish the bread
    before there is none,

discover each other before
    we leave,

and enjoy each other for what we are
    while we have the time.

                Amen.

CHAPTER 5

The Holy Wars

Since the first battle between Cain and Abel, wars have been waged for both noble and ignoble purposes. Among the bloodiest were those of the Middle Ages when knights sallied forth in search of the Holy Grail.

I've never known what a Holy Grail was, but I figured it must have been pretty important if people fought over it. On second thought, if you asked me to recall what my brother and I were fighting about on December 14, 1952, I wouldn't have the foggiest notion. But I know it seemed pretty important to me at the time.

One thing I do know, in those days people justified massacres and other human injustices for what they called "Christian" causes. (The actions of those warriors were seldom Christlike as our history books will attest.)

I think of those Holy Wars and I find myself asking, "Is there any connection between those wars of the Middle Ages and spiritual battles in homes today? Have we Christians justified the use of any means, no-holds-barred, to produce a desired end?"

As soldiers in spiritual warfare, we tend to think every situation requires drastic measures. We rush around like the conscientious person in a "Raid" commercial. (Get this sin out of here...**ssssst!**) In the process, we lose our sense of humor. Every tiny speck becomes a boulder.

Unfortunalely, because we think our situation is serious, we have a tendency to select an approach of "cannon intensity." Just think of trying to shoot a cannonball through a Kleenex and you'll see the humor in selecting the wrong intensity of weapon.

In order to tell one opponent from another, perhaps a chart will help us.

Some people are clearly one type. Others are a mixture of two or three types. Do you know which one you are? Maybe you would want to add another category, more accurately describing yourself, to the list on the left.

On the right you'll find a list of traits that might belong to your loved one. Depending on how polarized the two sides are, you can fairly well predict whether the battles will be waged with slingshot or cannon.

WHO'S AT ODDS WITH WHOM?

1. **Strong Traditional**
   "My church is the right one. We have the **right** doctrine."

2. **Defensive Person**
   "I don't like to lose arguments. I can't let others see me as being in the wrong."

3. **Die-Hard Evangelist**
   "I've brought five people to the Lord this week. Even if I have to burn out in the process, I'm gonna keep winning souls to Christ."

4. **The Eternal Campaigner**
   Tendency to be on some soapbox. This time it's religion.

5. **The Great Awakening**
   (Teen or older)
   Usually has had a moving "experience" at the time of conversion. Wants others to have the same.

THE SCRIMMAGE LINE

1. **Free Thinker**
   (Unbeliever)
   "Nobody's going to tell **me** what to believe. I'm my own person."

2. **Violent Type**
   (Unbeliever)
   "Get out of my life; and take your #*! religion with you."

3. **Ho-Hum Nominal**
   "I go to church every Sunday. You don't need all that extra stuff during the week Too many prayer groups and you'll become a fanatic!"

4. **Take it or Leave it**
   (Unbeliever)
   "You can talk about religion if you want, but I can't get too excited about that stuff."

5. **Sideliner**
   (Counterfeit believer)
   "I go to church on Christmas and Easter."

6. **The Late Bloomer**
   Found Christ as an adult. Intense in concern that loved ones won't find Christ in time.

7. **The Spiritually Ravenous**
   Can't get enough of church-related activities, Bible studies, prayer groups, etc.

—THE SCRIMMAGE LINE—

6. **Separatist**
   "You take care of your spiritual needs and let me take care of mine."

7. **Slow-to-Grow**
   (Believer)
   "Grow? Not necessary. If you're saved that's all you need."

   or

   Huff-huff-pant-pant
   "I'm growing as fast as I can. I can't keep up with your expectations for me. **Help!**"

Now let's take a look at the following scene. As you read it, if you're one who likes to underline passages, and if this is your book, underline those portions which suggest to you that either party is throwing up a blockade or smoke screen. While you're at it, ask yourself, "Have I ever done that to anybody?" (As I did this myself, every page overflowed with underlines aplenty.) You may be able to pick up a few applications to situations in your life which have proved frustrating.

———————

Betty (not her real name) had been reared in a Christian home. At the age of 14 she became aware of Jesus in a personal way. Her upbringing had been strict, full of rules and expectations befitting her age and the moral environment her parents had chosen for her.

Once out of school and off to college, she began to try some new things—some things she was sure her parents would have raised an eyebrow over, had they known about them.

But she emerged from college days relatively un-scathed, and with a handsome young man at her side. Ben, an athletic hero on campus, was popular with everyone. Betty and Ben liked many of the same things, and seemed a good match for each other. But, in all those hours they sat under the campus oak trees, joking and laughing, Betty had never broached the subject of religion. She was certain that love would conquer all. She told herself, "He loves me. He'll come around."

Shortly before graduation, Ben proposed, and Betty was delirious. Not only a diploma in June, but a diamond as well! Betty knew her parents would ask, "Is Ben a Christian?" She also knew she couldn't give them a clear answer. Ben was a good person, kind, loving...surely that counted heavily, too. She hoped that would be enough for her parents.

It wasn't enough. They objected. They weren't violent about it, but their comments did put Betty on the defensive. She felt like someone had sat on her birthday cake.

Being headstrong and full of optimism, Betty decided to go ahead and marry Ben regardless of her parents' feelings. Ben had said, "I won't object to your religion. You can go to church and who knows, maybe I'll come with you sometimes. We can work things out. Just don't bug me about it."

Encouraged, Betty hummed a tune of counterfeit optimism. "I know I can change him, in time."

Autumn came and they were married in the chapel on campus. Betty's parents came, though her mother had to do considerable maneuvering to get Betty's father to give the bride away. Betty's paternal grandmother refused to come at all.

Determined to prove everyone wrong, Betty worked overtime to build up Ben's profile in the eyes of her family. Her parents liked Ben; they just had reservations about the future.

But Betty soft-pedaled religion. In fact, for the first

year she went to church only occasionally. It seemed easier than throwing cold water on Sunday morning plans Ben may have made. She wanted to keep things peaceful.

Three years after they were married, their first child was born. Two years after that, another. Now, her religious roots stirred; Betty wanted to get back into church. She wanted her children to have the same rich heritage of Christmas pageants, Easter sunrise services and baptisms that she had.

When she told Ben of her desire to take the children to Sunday school, he said, "Why not let them grow up and then decide for themselves?" But Betty persisted so Ben softened. In the back of her mind Betty thought, "Who knows, maybe the children's attending will make it easier to reach Ben."

Ben showed no interest in their Sunday morning routine of getting dressed up for church. Betty pretended they were going to a gala celebration; Ben pretended to sleep through the racket.

One Sunday, she nudged Ben. "Why don't you come to church with me and the children? It would be good for you."

Ben's reaction was clear. "I'd rather sleep in on Sundays. It's the only time I have off."

Betty, feeling rebuffed, took the children by the hand and briskly marched them to the car. When she returned from church, she wore a mask of straight-lipped reserve. For the remainder of the day her replies were short, crisp and curt. Somehow, she reasoned, Ben needed to know he'd disappointed her.

Betty did not let Ben's early remarks thwart her in continuing the children's spiritual training. With the passing weeks, she introduced table grace and bedtime prayers.

Ben didn't object, but it was obvious he felt uncomfortable when spiritual matters were spotlighted.

Occasionally Betty would invite him to functions at

church: couples-club dinners, family outings, Sunday school picnics. Only once did he accompany her. Upon returning home he announced, "I really don't like those affairs. I hope you won't ask me to go any more."

While other couples and their children sat in pews together, she found herself remembering the times she had attended services with her parents. How she had loved the potluck suppers and the old-fashioned "hymn sings" that followed. And the times they asked the pastor and his wife home for Sunday dinners. She missed those family church activities.

Betty began to feel increasingly embarrassed as a "solo parent" at church. Eventually she became so sensitive about being alone, she manufactured excuses for Ben's absence. Friends unwittingly added pressure when they inquired, "Do you think Ben would like to come to Bible study on Sunday evenings?" How did **she** know if he would **ever** come to Bible study, or church, or anything?

She confronted Ben one Sunday as he sat at the breakfast table, unshaven, reading the morning paper.

"You don't want me to go to church, do you?" Her eyes flashed with rage. She barely realized that she had passed judgment and was putting words in his mouth.

"No, I didn't say that. I'm just saying count me out. I don't intend to become a Christian. It's as simple as that."

Betty walked away, her banner of martyrdom flying high.

That night, as she lay in bed, she replayed the day's experience in her mind—his responses, her responses, the responses she wished she'd been brilliant enough to make. With each replay, more juices of antagonism and hurt flowed.

As time went by, she turned with increasing frequency to the solace and comfort of Bible studies and prayer groups.

As a wife trying alone to hold her family together spiritually, she found herself taking over, pulling the children close. She wanted them to look to her, rather than to Ben, for principles of living.

Now she became aware of a belligerent spouse, who inwardly stewed whenever "Jesus" or "church" entered a conversation.

Betty stewed, too. She often felt like a hypocrite. "I'm a Christian. I shouldn't feel this way or entertain such hateful feelings." And then guilt would set in.

Betty knew her inner convictions and yearnings for the things of God could not be shelved. To give up church completely and pull the children out of Sunday school would keep peace in the family, but she knew the problem could not be solved that easily. Somehow, she and Ben had to learn to live with their differences without slamming each other's values.

Betty recognized she needed new insight into coping with the spiritual imbalances in their relationship. But she had to convince Ben they needed help. She didn't want this "thing" eating away at the core of what started out to be a good marriage.

In considering a counselor Ben would listen to, she recognized a Christian counselor would be her choice but not his. So she encouraged Ben to consider someone in family services, someone who wouldn't wear a funny collar, or have a picture of Jesus behind his office chair.

Ben agreed to counseling. He realized their marriage had a lot going for it, and he, too, felt it was foolish to let this one area erode future happiness. He was willing to try.

The counselor met separately with each mate for some sessions and jointly for others.

During a session with Betty alone, one of the questions he asked was: "How badly do you want to hang on to old ways of responding?"

The counselor pointed out that clinging to moods was one of the subtlest of manipulations. It becomes a power play in which one person says, "You hurt me, so now we will both suffer. I'm not going through this alone." Betty needed to realize she could be turning her husband away from herself, as well as from the God she so desperately wanted him to embrace.

The counselor asked another question: "How much do your husband's feelings and desires count for?"

Both of them had experienced an upsurge of old childhood memories when their children came along. What had seemed right for each person's own childhood was projected toward the desire for that person's children...independent of what the other marital partner felt.

Betty thought, "Religion was good for me when I was growing up. I want my children to have the same rich experiences."

Ben, on the other hand, held the contrasting view. "Well, I turned out okay, didn't I? I never had religion as a kid and my children don't need it either."

The phrase that describes the above situation is **hidden agenda.** Besides the hidden agendas Betty and Ben each entertained for their children, they also had hidden agendas for programming each other. It had been so long since either had said, "You know, honey, on a scale of one to ten, this thing on Sunday is a nine for me. I really want to go." Instead, they had become reactionaries to nebulous or completely unnamed expectations.

Betty's counselor helped her ask herself:

Does my happiness depend on what others say or do?

Do my moods depend on the opinions others have of my beliefs? Does their judgment affect my ability to function?

Do I find myself accepting others only if they are Christians?

Think about your own situation for a moment. How would you answer the same questions? A Christian counselor I know explains to his patients, "Happiness is an internal reaction—a response to the Christ dwelling within. It is not dependent upon circumstances, and often operates independently from outward situations."

To put that into everyday language: A man **without Christ** is like a sailor in a tiny boat floundering in an Atlantic storm. **With Christ,** the man becomes like the captain of a submarine—the waves are still crashing overhead, but beneath the surface things are calm. The captain's faith acts as a buffer.

Betty was like the sailor in the little rowboat. In her attempt to tame the elements, she made the erroneous assumption that she could change Ben. But it didn't work. And the more he balked, the more she pushed. She eventually became angry at not being in control of the situation, and she directed that anger toward Ben. She would say, "It's his fault I feel this way."

Adam and Eve started the first finger-pointing in the Garden of Eden. The pattern has continued for centuries. In Betty's case she was simply deceiving herself.

Another thing Betty's counselor cautioned her about was re-hashing Ben's transgressions, real or imagined. The counselor advised her to avoid the temptation to relate upsetting events indiscriminately to her friends. Repetition reinforces, and a vicious circle is established when negative feelings and experiences are expressed again and again.

What could Betty do when she was tempted to rerun the video tapes of her mind? She could discipline herself to do something totally unrelated...like jog around the block, clean a cupboard or play a sonata on her cello. Without such healthy outlets, she could continue to feed the seeds of an unforgiving heart. And the end result of that might well be mental stress to the point of mental illness.

During one session when both Betty and Ben were present, the counselor addressed the subject of alienation. How do people alienate one another?

One way, he suggested, was to imply, "See what a good time I'm having without you!" Betty and Ben had each been guilty of that. For Ben, it was a round or two of golf on Sunday morning. When he'd come in he'd be sure to be very animated about the good time he had been having. Betty did the same thing when she came back from meetings at the church.

The counselor explained this "game" was actually a jealousy ploy. Ben and Betty really needed to find ways of reassuring each other, instead of resorting to a tug of war.

Fidelity was another word that came up in the discussions. It became apparent that Betty needed to consider the regular conferences she had been having with her pastor.

Was she going to him because he could help her produce a desired change in Ben? Was she searching for ways to change herself and her spiritual paralysis? Or, was she going to him as a way of saying, "Ben, you don't satisfy my spiritual needs, but Pastor does"? In other words, were her visits to her pastor honorable?

It turned out that in Ben's view she was committing a sort of spiritual adultery. "She knows I can't give her the spiritual companionship she would like, so she goes elsewhere. I wouldn't mind, if she didn't flaunt it."

Ben discussed some other needs. He felt his masculinity and his position as the head of the house were eroding. Betty, he professed, was usurping authority and denying him opportunities to lead his family. Whenever she'd whisk the children aside to give them moral teaching, he'd think, "What's the matter with me? I'm capable of teaching the kids a few things about right and wrong. I'm no dummy." Ben wanted to be included in those sessions, so long as Betty didn't put him on the spot with Bible quizzes.

Betty, on the other hand, didn't feel he could possibly teach the children the **right** values. After all, he wasn't a Christian.

As we reflect upon the story of Betty and Ben, it becomes apparent that keeping doors of communication open may be the only chance for their marriage to survive.

Interestingly, some of the counsel from the secular world was able to minister to the spiritual problem between them. Even though their counselor was not a Christian, he was part of God's plan in helping Betty and Ben.

I'm sure you're hoping that I can now impress you with a fairy-tale ending: a lovely couple going off hand in hand into the sunset.

If I could say to you, "Six months later Ben was converted and is now teaching a Sunday school class," you'd smile and think, now wasn't that a nice ending? Then you'd think about your situation and you'd say, "I'm trying like Betty. Why isn't it working out for me? I've been waiting 20 years." You might even get an attack of the "guilties."

So I'm not going to tell you that.

I think their actual progress report will prove more helpful.

I've never seen a couple work as hard at building a trusting relationship as Ben and Betty are. And something tells me that **that** will minister more to Ben and make him more receptive to the love of God than anything else. I think they're going to make it, don't you?

CHAPTER 6

Coming Home
After A Spiritual High

Have you ever met anyone who has had a Saul-of-Tarsus-type conversion? Or maybe one who has taken a 180° turn-around and is now an energetic dynamo for the cause of Christ?

I know of a family in California—the Taylors, I'll call them—who had always hoped their children would be able to pass through the turbulent teen years without abandoning their morals or the practice of churchgoing. In 1967, their son Ron, who had been having some difficulties in school, agreed to attend a church retreat in the mountains near Santa Cruz. When he returned from the two-day affair he glowed like a light bulb.

Ron's mother was pleased he had had such a good time, but soon she began to voice misgivings. When I asked her how it was going, she raised her eyebrows. "The whole house is in an uproar. Since Ron 'got religion' he's driving us crazy. First, it was listening to the spiritual 'truths' as he called them. Then there were the tracts and books he started bringing home. Nyla, I wonder if he's becoming a 'Jesus freak.'"

Sometimes new believers go through a "honeymoon phase," and there's never any guarantee of the kind of Christian a person will become after a conversion experience. But Marge and Bill Taylor hadn't expected anything like this.

As the weeks went by, Ron took an increasingly active part in activities at church. During "Youth Sunday," he

55

and another boy even delivered mini-sermons. All were impressed that such a new Christian could speak with so much conviction and forcefulness. Ron's hat size increased.

But the real scrimmage lines formed between Ron and his father. Bill Taylor had put up with two, and then three, religious bumper stickers on the family car—all affixed without asking anyone. He'd lived with the new wave of Christian rock music and spiritual folk song records. He'd closed one eye to the slogan buttons parading across Ron's Sunday morning dress shirt.

But he couldn't abide Ron's growing insensitivity. Ron delivered his ex cathedra sermonettes with increasing regularity and superiority. Bill Taylor had been heard to say, "You'd think Ron doesn't count us among the saved and forgiven."

Ron had done everything but call his dad a "fall-away." He didn't realize that abandoning old traits or bad habits doesn't always come instantly with the salvation package. Ron's list of "oughts," things a Christian ought to do, unfortunately was really a long list of ought **not's.**

He'd see his dad have a cigar now and then, or he'd hear him tell a slightly off-color joke, and he'd say to himself, "But my dad goes to church every Sunday and says he's a Christian." And he would be quick to tell his father, "A **true** Christian wouldn't tell those kinds of stories."

Bill, embarrassed and outraged by his son's sudden assumption of a fatherly role, would return the volley. "I'll do just as I please, young man. Whether he's got religion or not, no son of mine is going to tell **me** how to live."

Under other circumstances, Bill Taylor, with the help of the Holy Spirit, might have tried to do something about his God-displeasing actions. But to have such things come from his son was simply too much, even though he did give some thought to what Ron had said.

What could Ron have done to bridge the growing gap?

First, he needed to realize that his father was as much a "baby Christian" as he was—in spite of their ages. Then he could have forgiven the inconsistencies he saw. If asked, he would have denied he was passing judgment on the salvation status of his father, but his actions were doing just that.

An excessive upsurge in Christian intensity can happen to anyone. When I first began this book, a pastor told me, "Be sure you include a chapter about a wife returning home after a Christian retreat." He had an amused look with a hint of a smile. Why, I wondered, was he smiling?

Then another pastor told me of a wife who came home from a retreat, aglow with renewal and bursting with enthusiasm. As she related the deep spiritual truths she had gleaned from the weekend, she added, "Honey, we're going to sweep the country with these spiritual concepts." The husband looked up with, "I hope you start with the kitchen!"

I had to admit I could relate to that story. Attending retreats and seminars was one of my favorite activities a few years ago. But I was never judicious in what I shared. I recall one incident of exuberance that produced a stalemate between Jerry and me. I rushed into the family room on a Sunday afternoon. Jerry was sitting with glazed eyes before the TV watching a Steelers-Dolphins football game; the Sunday paper was scattered on the floor.

Still "high" from the retreat, I was eager to share my experience and I just knew he, being a Christian, would be interested.

"Hi, honey...I'm home," I called out. After a dutiful kiss on his cheek, I launched into my story. "I can't tell you how much this weekend has meant to me. I feel like a different person. I **am** a different person, you'll see."

He monotoned, "Fine, fine. I'll be with you as soon as they finish this play."

I stood boxed in like a race horse at the starting gate.

From the corner of my eye, I saw the play was over. I began again, but his shushing finger to the lips told me I was still premature.

He leaned forward, his arms tense, hands clasped.

"Boy, that Terry Bradshaw can really handle the ball."

My fire was rapidly being quenched. I began again. "I've learned so much, but I don't know where to start."

Jerry turned down the sound on the TV. His eyes seemed distracted, as if he were lipreading each play. By the furrowed brow, I could tell he was not finding this arrangement satisfactory.

In ten minutes I attempted to relate everything I had learned in two days. His gaze was emotionless. My mind murmured, "Is he being polite and patronizing? Is he silently disagreeing with my every word? Is he hoping I'll finish so he can get back to his game? Is he silently accusing me of flaunting my spirituality?" I couldn't decide and I was afraid to ask. Then I saw a steely "enough is enough" look, and I quickly found a graceful way to terminate the conversation.

Wandering through the house to hang up my coat, I dropped all my notes on the floor. While trying to assemble them in respectable order, I heard Jerry from the other room. "Get 'em, get 'em!" All I could think of was, "I don't care who gets whom. My welcome home wasn't anything like I'd planned."

What went wrong? You probably spotted the trouble points from the start.

1. I didn't seem to care what Jerry was doing when I came in, so he was not interested in my retreat—at least, not then.

2. I didn't ask him how he had fared in my absence or I would have known he burned the Friday supper and had to send out for replacements; the dog wandered into the swamp twice and had to be bathed after each episode; Jerry was not comfortable with the role of businessman-turned-housekeeper.

3. It never occurred to me that it would be impossible for him to enter into my retreat experience.

4. I was insensitive and unconcerned as to the right time to tell him about my weekend.

Husbands react in different ways to the women who return from retreats or religious experiences. Some are impressed; some are turned off; some are apathetic.

I've heard of wives who returned so transformed that their husbands were awed by the changes and later coveted the same experiences for themselves.

It does happen, but it is not common. More often, men will see the spiritual glow, but pride stops them from pursuing the issue further. Sometimes they notice the glow but mistake it for a searchlight and run from it.

It is hard to see positive changes if we try to force our loved ones to reach what we believe to be our own level. I plead guilty to that one, because I saw what my intensity could do to my steady, easygoing husband.

I was a striver, eager to get the most spiritual growth in the shortest span of time. I couldn't understand why he didn't run at my speed, especially if he were a true Christian.

The most valuable lesson in God's notebook under the heading, "How To Teach Nyla Not To Push So Hard" began on the last morning of one seminar I attended.

The pastor's opening comments that morning were something like this: "Most of you should be home right now. You've been lectured to death and have acquired so much heavenly information you're likely to strangle your husband with spirituality when you get home."

Then he began to pray, "Lord, send them home with a godly humbling so they can love their husbands rather than teach them."

That was the start of a new and more subdued Nyla. How did it happen?

The pastor-lecturer was a world-renowned speaker; his charisma was appealing and his messages forceful. He said, "I have always been a deeply religious man. I married, began my ministry and watched the fruit of my labor expand for the Lord. I felt so close to God, I thought I was on the top rung of a ladder peeking into heaven.

"With so much happening in my spiritual growth, I was eager to tell my wife everything. At first, when I told Dorothy about my experiences, she was interested. The more I grew, the more I wanted to grow. And the more I wanted to share it with her.

"But as time passed, I noticed my wife becoming more withdrawn. We were beginning to experience communication problems.

"Then one day as I was studying in my office, I sensed God's presence. 'Why do you constantly call Dorothy to join you on the higher rungs of your spiritual ladder?' God seemed to say.

"I answered, 'It's so great to fellowship with you, Lord. I just want Dorothy to be a part of it.'

"'Do you really care for Dorothy?' God said.

"'You know I do.'

"'Then go down to her place on the ladder.'"

The audience's muffled gasp, including my own, indicated a lesson had hit our spiritually haughty hearts.

He continued. "As I sat in my study, I found myself turning pages in my Bible. My eyes fell upon Philippians 2:6-8. All my years of study had revealed this passage to demonstrate the ultimate in humility:

"'Who, being in the form of God, thought it not robbery to be equal with God: But made Himself of no reputation, and took upon Him the form of a servant, and was made in the likeness of men: And being found in fashion as a man, He humbled Himself and became obedient unto death, even the death of the cross' (KJV).

"As my eyes absorbed those words," he said, "God's Holy Spirit revealed something new and fresh to me. Jesus enjoyed His position at the top of the ladder. He was as close to the Father as anyone could get. It must have been the ultimate of all spiritual experiences. In a small measure, I was enjoying my relationship with God in the same way.

"When I thought of all He gave up in order to take on

the mortality of manhood, it brought tears to my eyes. I realized then God wanted me to see how Christ had come down the ladder to identify with me and with all humanity.

"Then I thought about my wife, Dorothy. Did I love her enough to go down to her place on the ladder and then be willing to make the climb with her? I knew I had to do something because my heart told me my wife was beginning to regress in her spirituality. I was gone a lot of the time on speaking engagements and when I was home I wanted to discuss my spiritual highs. But Dorothy was struggling to keep afloat, managing the three children, the house, the finances—things I found mundane compared with God's work.

"So I stopped everything and stayed home for six months. I maintained my devotions and study, but not at the expense of my wife and children. I didn't know I had such great kids. And Dorothy...well, she became a true helpmate and partner. It wasn't easy, but I counted the cost and decided I was willing to pay the price for balance in our lives."

I felt tears rushing to my eyes as the pastor finished. God's Holy Spirit was making the first incision of spiritual surgery in my life.

All the way home, my eyes puddled. Sometimes I could barely see the road. One thing kept running through my mind: If Jesus humbled Himself for me, couldn't I do the same for Jerry? I knew I had to cease my rushing ahead.

Finally a prayer came to my lips, a prayer I would repeat every day for over a year. **Lord, bring me to the place where Jerry and I can approach You together.**

What agonies I endured that year! I experienced poor health, which prevented me from attending many meetings. I had spent hours poring over religious magazines and testimony books—often at the expense of daily Bible reading, and that had to be moderated. It was as painful as giving up desserts.

Relationships that had satisfied me before became empty. Friends couldn't empathize with my problems, so I grew to depend on them less and less.

Then came periods of introspection. I told myself, "Nyla, you're not real. You're so 'spiritual' others can't relate to you...you only tell the victories; you never share the defeats. You carelessly cast aside others' doubts or lack of faith. You're a self-righteous windbag."

I was beginning to think I needed to see a psychiatrist.

At night I'd go to bed and begin conversations with Jerry that I couldn't finish. Emptiness again. I'd cry myself to sleep, thinking myself to be a failure.

Then I asked God, **Help me see and hear myself as others see me.** The answer to that prayer came through a turned-tables incident.

A friend had gone on a retreat and had phoned me the next day. She was absolutely bubbling and animated. She said, "If you could go on one of these fabulous retreats, **then** we'd really be like sisters in Christ," **Then?** Wait a minute, I thought, aren't we already sisters in Christ? Is she telling me I'm no longer her sister, or that perhaps I never was?

I was confused and hurt. A wedge had been shoved between us, impairing what I had considered a compatible relationship. (Did Jerry ever feel that way when I came home extolling my experiences?) Ah, the pain of my moment of truth. My thoughts quickly bounced from my friend to Jerry, then back to my friend again:

Did I love her enough to overlook her remarks? (Had Jerry loved me enough to overlook my steamroller tactics and subtle accusations that maybe he wasn't the Christian he thought he was?)

What would I do now? How would I keep the channel of communication open between my friend and me? (Will there come a time in my marriage when Jerry won't have the patience to put up with my trying to remold him? Will he someday not care, and will the channels of communication close?)

What about your situation? When you returned to the dorm or your place of work exhilarated from a spiritual retreat, workshop weekend or seminar, did you rave about spiritual truths in double-exclamation-point intensity, only to have your roommates or co-workers show polite lack of interest?

Have you said, "If you'd only come with me, you could have this too"? Some people show interest and you may get a few takers—but at what cost? How about the rest of them?

But wait, I must be fair. Some enthusiasm and sharing **must** happen after profound awakenings. Think about the early church. After Pentecost and the sharing that took place that day, many others were drawn by the enthusiasm.

The trouble with those of us who have outgoing personalities is that our energy levels seem amplified after conversion or renewal. An underdeveloped "feedback" system with friends or family is like a person wearing earphones while trying to talk to others in the room. The speaker begins to shout, but is unaware of his loudness because he can't hear the sound of his own voice.

If you can stand the honesty, I'd suggest you ask of someone to whom you've been witnessing, "Do I come on too strong sometimes?"

Risk asking.

That step may be the key to opening the door for genuine spiritual sharing. Your vulnerability may do wonders for your relationship with that other person.

———————

Lord, I suspect I come on strong at inappropriate times. Help me to hear myself as others hear me. Soothe my bruised ego and heal the scars in the relationships in which I've been overbearing. I want so much to share my experiences. Help me moderate my exuberance to Your glory. Amen.

CHAPTER 7

Household Plants

When I began the rough draft of this book some time ago, I decided to interview, man-on-the-street style, the most important human being in my life—my husband.

Jerry was accustomed to a wife whose creative juices produced novel ways of approaching tasks, so I knew he would not be surprised by this means of gathering information.

One night, while Jerry was changing into his after-work clothes, I sat cross-legged on our bed with notebook in hand and pen poised.

"Jerry, pretend I'm interviewing you about the subject of this new book I'm doing. I need an unemotional, unbiased opinion."

He smiled, proceeded to loosen his tie, and gave me a quizzical look. "Go ahead. Fire away."

"Ahem!" (I cleared my throat to change the scene from a wife talking to her husband to a professional journalist awaiting a hot tip.)

"Mr. Witmore, tell me, when did you first become aware that I...er...I mean, your wife was plotting to improve your spirituality?"

His reply came immediately, much to my surprise. I had envisioned him scratching his chin, looking upward to retrieve a memory from the ceiling, and otherwise struggling for an astute reply. Instead, I got an athlete ready to charge at the sound of the gun.

"The first thing that comes to mind are the books and literature she'd leave around the house."

"Did you read any of it?" (Finally I was going to find out if my "tract plants"—literature planted around the house—had had any effect.)

"Well, I read some, but it didn't make any difference. She was too obvious."

I lost my identity for a moment. "I was?...er, you mean it was too conspicuous? You weren't fooled?"

I rolled back on the bed, flopping both arms spread-eagle fashion. "And I thought I was so subtle!"

Jerry and I both started to laugh, a healthy refreshing chuckle that mushroomed into a howl. It was the first time we had been able to laugh about a hard time in our marriage. What release!

Let me tell you how I got started in the subversiveness of pamphlet-planting.

In my earliest recollections, I had heard stories of persons who used tracts successfully. I figured out there were two reasons to use a tract: First, the tracts can say it better than you. Second, it's the coward's way out.

Realizing my nature has always been somewhat non-confronting, I thought tracts and pamphlets were the perfect way. So I proceeded to pollinate the countryside, like a spiritual Johnny Appleseed. Often I was too bashful even to ask permission but just left tracts in doctors' offices and other public places anyway.

Later, I began to carry a heavy purse with lots of zippered compartments. Into each I stuffed small tracts and paperback books hoping for an opportunity to introduce a piece here or there on buses or planes as I traveled.

I was armed with ammunition to cover a variety of circumstances. When I tried to work up to a presentation, though, my mouth would go dry and the articulations would sound like two pieces of Velcro tape being torn apart! It was very distracting.

Normally, tracts, books and pamphlets serve a valuable purpose. They provide an orderly, concise means of presenting spiritual truths. They educate and enlighten a reader, whether or not the reader embraces the message of the tract. Sometimes the reader finds Christ; at other times the material serves only to irritate or annoy. You never know how another person will respond.

I recall only one instance in which I used a tract with

absolute success. It came about in response to a scrawled note at the bottom of our annual Christmas newsletter. To my friend Angie I had written these words, "Since Jerry and I have discovered God's priorities for our lives, it has made all the difference in the world."

Not long thereafter I got a long-distance call from Angie. "What did you mean by that note in your letter? I've got to know."

"Read what I said; then I'll tell you." She read the note to me, and I began to explain it.

"Angie, when I was growing up I remembered all the Christmas songs about Jesus dying for the people of the world. It seemed so far away. But I always understood that Jesus' job was to bring reconciliation between man and God. Jesus takes our failures and sins on His shoulders so that we won't have to carry them around any longer."

"Yes, I believe that too, Nyla."

"Well, salvation, in its general sense, is for all mankind. It's for everybody who wants it. But it's not enough to know that Jesus died for the whole world's sins. That isn't personal enough. There came a time in my life when I knew I needed to be convinced that Jesus died for Nyla. So I asked God to make that miracle happen in my life."

"How did you do that?"

"I simply asked God to do what was necessary to convince me that Jesus was everything the Bible said He was. One day I discovered that I really believed it was true, and I was convinced that Jesus was more than a great teacher or prophet. I knew that I wanted His presence to stay with me forever. That was when it became personal for me. That was the moment that Jesus became my Savior; but that wasn't the end of it. There was one more thing I needed."

"What was that?"

"I went on for a number of years with Jesus as my Savior but not as my Lord."

"I don't understand. What do you mean by Lord?"

"Lordship is the degree to which you let Christ control and guide your everyday affairs. It means that you and I need to let Him be boss instead of insisting on our own way."

"Hmmmmm," I heard her say on the other end of the line.

"Angie," I said, "are you sure you've got all those ingredients? It's the key to help you understand the difference between your priorities and God's."

Angie then began to ask me to lead her towards finding that kind of assurance. I wasn't sure how to go about praying for these steps, and I'd never had much experience praying over the telephone, but I asked her to bear with me while I went to get a small tract that contained just the prayers she needed. I began reading and when we finished with the tract she gave the biggest sigh.

"Oh, I've never felt this way before. I thought I knew, but I didn't really have the assurance. I feel like a bunch of light bulbs have just been turned on. Wow!"

If I could have hugged Angie over the phone line, I would have. So many times I had wanted to tell her about my faith but had avoided it for fear of becoming embroiled in an argument over theology. Now everything came together in clear order. This was the time Angie's need and my witness were meant to connect directly with God's throne.

One of the things that strikes me about that conversation is that I sensed Angie's direct need, and I was able to forget my usual self-consciousness. At another time, I might have barged into a witnessing situation and ended up arguing over Bible verses to defend my position. There was none of that in this conversation.

Do you yearn to be able to share more naturally? Would you like to be free of self-consciousness when you share your faith? Ask God to show you the times you don't have to force things to happen.

When you try to force something...you lose much of your effectiveness. Here are some questions to ask yourself:

1. "Am I trying to manipulate another's spiritual experiences?" Manipulation goes beyond the simple desire to inform. It wants to remold another person's life, often for selfish gain. For example, why do I want to change my loved one? So he or she will treat me better?

2. "Am I so emotionally involved that I tend to rush prematurely into witnessing situations?"

3. "Have I been guilty of thinking the end justifies the means?" Do I say, it doesn't matter how I get my loved one interested in spiritual things, even if I have to use subversive plotting and devious ploys?

4. "Do I find myself using manipulative means to witness, and afterward sink into despondency or depression when the method doesn't work?" If that is happening, you are forgetting that your job is to be the seed-planter. It is the Holy Spirit's job to convince, not yours. You don't close the sale. He does.

5. "Do I react nervously when another person rejects my sharing? Am I defensive?" If you are, your listener will feel you are trying to sell something, rather than share it.

6. "Am I presenting my case casually?" Take pains to develop your ability to respond casually too. It is far better to have a reaction that suggests, "I care more about you than I do this material, or being right about this issue."

7. "Do I use pamphlets as spiritual 'whips'?" Don't shove a book under another person's nose in a you-had-better-read-this-or-else fashion. Likewise, avoid passing pamphlets that suggest, "I have all the right answers," or "I told you so—you're wrong and I'm right." By proving someone else is wrong, you may win the battle but lose the war.

8. "Can I recognize the times I ought to keep quiet?" I believe there are times you should choose to remain

silent, even if you are likely to be seen as being in the wrong. Jesus chose to be silent before His accusers just before His crucifixion. There are times when silence will speak louder and more effectively than speaking or giving a book. When you walk closely with God's Spirit, you know the difference.

"Household plants" may work well for some. But I should caution you to re-examine your intentions. It is dishonest to deceive. Deception seeds take root quickly and grow up as weeds.

If others are to find Christ or a re-awakening of their faith, let it be because they discovered a book you actually misplaced or left lying around. Let love be genuine and without guilt.

Father, if I've been dishonest in placing materials for others' eyes to fall upon, convict me of it now. If I've hidden my faith for fear it would be trampled upon, remind me of those times. Like Peter who denied You three times, forgive me for thinking more about my self-image than about genuine openness in sharing what You've done for me. Affirm my worth like You did for Peter. Let me know You can still use me to feed Your sheep. Amen.

CHAPTER 8

From Household Plants to a Moment of Truth

This chapter was the hardest one to write. It is painful to relive times I'm not proud of. But for credibility's sake, I must make myself transparent...just as I had to do with Jerry.

What do I hope to accomplish by such honesty?

First, I think it will help you counsel others who are inclined to be excessive and harmful in their well-meant efforts to reach loved ones for Christ.

Second, if you are the overzealous offender, you may learn something from my mistakes and find a calming from God's Spirit that will make you far more effective than you presently are.

Yes, those of us who have what I call "the urge to surge" can learn to share faith without putting up roadblocks. It is possible. And it's easier when you're committed to restraining the urge to push God or play Holy Spirit.

By nature, I've always been a rusher...Nyla-in-a-hurry. In the past, others have had to tell me when I was striving too hard. Now I've learned to sense it for myself. I think I'm growing up, but it wasn't until my mid-thirties that I found out how to do it. God used my marriage to teach me.

Jerry and I were both raised in homes where church-going was not an unusual activity. But like many young couples starting out, we did other things on Sundays during the first year of our marriage. We enjoyed skiing, went away on weekends, slept in. Jerry had lost the churchgoing habit during his days in the military. And I? Well, I had rebelled after my college graduation, having spent too much time with people who were skeptical of Christianity. However, in spite of our falling away, early experiences had been recorded and the memory tapes eventually would be played.

That time came following the birth of our first son. Now, we were a family, and we yearned to do the things we'd seen our families do. That included going to church.

During our courtship, Jerry and I had never discussed deep religious issues. Most discussions resulted in each of us taking opposing positions, whatever the subject: philosophy, education, politics, etc. I always saw issues as complex and Jerry saw them as simplistic and concrete. For all the many right things that bound us to each other, it was obvious we often held diametrically opposing views.

When we did start attending church again, we sat in the pew together—but that was it. No discussions of the sermons. No Bible studies. No prayer groups. No praying with each other except for grace at meals. I yearned for more. Church and table grace were not enough—not for me, at least.

My first big mistake—anyone's first big mistake—was thinking, "I'll change him." I figured unity in marriage meant thinking the same way and having the same experiences, holding similar values, liking the same things. I thought to be happy in the Christian sense, I'd have to make him become more like me. Since the religious issue was important to me, I felt Jerry should bend in my direction.

I didn't see that if one person loved to engage in intellectual and theological scrimmages while the other preferred a more relaxed approach, the difference was actually a matter of style. I was using a microscope while Jerry preferred the wide-angle lens; I was intense while

Jerry was conservative and casual. Obviously there's a need for both views in the body of believers, but I didn't see that at the time.

Our differences in style heightened about the eighth year of our marriage. It was then I experienced a renewal that was more intense than my conversion as a teenager. With that renewal came a whole new set of pressures. More than ever I wanted Jerry to jump on the wagon. But his feet were planted firmly in a Martin Luther stance: "Here I stand, I cannot do otherwise."

How can a spiritual renewal produce such polarization? I don't know about others, but I know that, for one thing, after mine my speech became liberally laced with "Praise the Lord" and "God is my whole life."

This renewal experience came to me while Jerry was away on a two-week business trip. I was seated in our living room one night, reading a book about a person whose life had been transformed during a quiet time with God. For some time I'd sensed a pulling toward God, particularly in the area of worship. I wanted to feel comfortable in God's presence. I wanted substance in my prayer life. For too long I had read off my "spiritual Christmas list," said, "Amen," and then darted off to play, do dishes or make beds.

How do you learn to feel comfortable telling God, "I love you"? This night I wanted to tell Him. I wanted to be able to remain silent in His presence without feeling awkward or filling the air with prideful requests. I decided I would not run away. This time I was going to sit, to do business with God on His terms, to stay until **He** dismissed me.

I closed my book, folded my hands and said nothing. Slowly, I began to praise Him. "Thank you, Lord, for being my Creator, for making the world, for sending Jesus, for giving me loving parents..." I thanked Him for all I know about Jesus, and for the times I had sensed His love and care for me. I thanked Him for the Holy Spirit. I thanked and thanked and thanked.

It was during those moments that Scripture fulfilled itself as promised in Psalm 22:3, "God inhabits the praises of His people." While I am sure that God has always been with me when I was praying, **this time** I was more worshipful and keenly aware of a tangible and loving presence in the room.

When I looked up, I noticed 45 minutes had passed. I could have continued for 45 more. That fact alone jarred me into realizing I was in the middle of something holy. Normally when I prayed, I'd start yawning or planning menus after only five or ten minutes.

Oh, how I wanted to tell Jerry. Right away. But he was 3,000 miles away and it hardly seemed right to disturb him in the middle of the night. I felt like a child with an "A" on a report card and no one at home to tell.

So, after quenching the desire to pick up the phone, I sat back in the chair and wondered, "Will Jerry think I've gone overboard emotionally? He's so calm and unemotional, and there's no way I can relate this happening in conservative, unemotional tones." I decided to face the issue when Jerry returned the following Friday.

Friday came. I thought by then the wind would be blowing more gently through my sails. Not so. With love's initial blush still on my cheeks, I recalled the days just after my experience. The grass was never greener, the sky never bluer and the sun never brighter. In a few short days I had become a dedicated Bible reader. Verses seemed literally to hop off the pages to attract my attention. That was the honeymoon phase, and I was in love with Jesus.

When Jerry returned I promised myself I'd wait for the right moment. I felt like a pregnant woman waiting to announce the news to the father-to-be. The right moment never materialized, though, and the pressure of bottled news began to build. I had the awful feeling I would not be able to release it in trickles.

More weeks went by—a sure sign of my cowardice, but also a sign that the Holy Spirit was not giving me a green light. Impatient, I finally took the matter into my own hands when Jerry gave me an obscure but optimistic sign. My slow drip became a gusher. Soon I was speaking like a 33⅓ r.p.m. record being played on a 45 r.p.m. turntable; even my voice pitch went up.

Besides that, I would normally have started at point A and moved to point B, C, D, and so on. Not this time. With machine-gun delivery, I started at point M, backtracked to A, jumped to P, Q, R, and ended with point B. Little wonder that Jerry was confused. I was making a big deal of something that should have been very straightforward. I didn't realize Jerry viewed me as a spiritual superior. He had always felt inadequate discussing the Bible with me because I had all my ammunition lined up...all the right Scriptures...all the right arguments. Who could discuss things with a know-it-all? My spiritual renewal (to him) was just one more reminder that I was above him on the spiritual ladder.

In my exuberance I was now unintentionally setting up stumbling blocks for the future. Without stopping to think that Jerry might misinterpret my experience, I wanted a pat on the back, a "Gee, I'm really happy for you," but in his eyes I saw uneasiness.

After that unsettling, one-sided conversation, I put a lid on further outbursts. Then I thought of "household plants"—Bibles, books, tracts and pamphlets. If I couldn't convince him with my own words, I'd use those of others to assure him I was no "weirdo." Instead of becoming enlightened, though, he was irritated that I kept the magazine racks full of my stuff.

Nevertheless, dreamer that I was, I planted our "library" with underlined Bibles, books with notes scrawled in the margins and an occasional tract that touted the advantages of the Spirit-filled life. Sometimes I'd set a book at a certain angle and later go back to check to see if it had been moved. If it hadn't, I'd toy with the idea of removing Jerry's magazines. Then he'd have no other choice. It is difficult to hop into Jerry's head and tell you how he reacted to all this. Since it was not his nature to analyze my every move, he was annoyed that I wasn't more direct.

It was the same way in conversation.

"What are you trying to say, Nyla?" he'd repeat over and over during my 10-minute build-ups. His confrontations always rattled me. I'd jump on the defensive and lose all rational thought. Using point M, J, K, L and then jumping back to B, I'd end up heaping confusion on top of confusion. I assumed Jerry could see where my details were heading. He couldn't. My main theme was always invisible.

Instead of asking, "Do you think we are growing in our faith?" I'd say, "Why don't you go to the Men's Club breakfast this Saturday?"

I'd ask every question but the right one. A direct question with a simple "yes" or "no" answer would have been so much better.

It seems a lot of married people waste so much time and energy playing games. They should be able to tell each other **anything**, right?

Here are some reasons I think some of us are so roundabout.

1. **Being married is no guarantee that we can or should tell everything.** Some spiritual things should be kept between us and God alone. Of those things we do choose to share, it is often difficult to know the depth and details that are appropriate or beneficial for our listeners.

2. **What happens to us personally tends to become magnified in our minds.** It is possible that what is important to us will not seem nearly so big to our listeners.

3. **We tend to forget that learning to communicate is a lifelong process.** We want instant success, but we have to feel our way slowly to determine the best ways to keep from overwhelming our listeners. It takes time, so don't flagellate yourself if you're a slow learner. Hang on.

4. We forget our loved ones are just as afraid to tell us their spiritual doubts as we are to tell ours.

5. We are so busy talking "at" each other we don't know how to talk "to" each other. (There are books and courses available to help. Ask your pastor or your Christian bookstore manager.)

6. We fail to see that human needs must often be met before a listener is willing to hear spiritual things.

Many of these reasons can be illustrated by an incident that happened to Jerry and me about seven years ago.

We were not aware that we had a serious communication problem until I recognized this fact: even though I was a former speech therapist, teacher and public speaker, I did not know everything about communication, especially with someone close to me.

One evening Jerry came home from work unusually tired. I could see he'd had a hard day as he pulled off his shoes and tie in slow motion. When he started to elaborate on the crises he'd faced, I felt an immediate urge to erase all negative comments by applying a spiritual answer. I interrupted him, "Let me show you what the Bible says about problems." I quickly quoted one or two verses that came to mind.

Suddenly Jerry looked at me icily. He carelessly threw his tie on the bed. "Nyla, the **last** thing in the world I need right now is a Bible verse."

I was shocked. This coming from my husband, a Christian? I wondered if he was losing his faith. Why else would he turn down one of my Bible-verse "band-aids"?

That was the problem. I was always quoting Bible verses to address various situations. You name it—I had a verse for it. But Bible memory verses were never meant to be used as spiritual whips to flog our listeners.

I was no more sensitive to Jerry than those who comfort the bereaved at funeral homes with a "Now, now, John's death was God's will." The point is that, while a Bible verse or the explanation "It's God's will" may be true, an old-fashioned hug might be more appropriate.

When a person is hurting, he needs to be comforted physically before he can be receptive to spiritual counsel. That is true whether you're dealing with unbelievers or Christians. Before a person is either of those, he is a human being.

Christ gave us that principle on a number of occasions. Remember how He healed the madman of

Gadara before He taught him? Repeatedly He met physical needs and used physical illustrations or parables before introducing the spiritual application and interpretation. Glance through your Bible and find the portions in Matthew, Mark, Luke and John where Christ dealt this way with people. You'll be amazed. For some reason, this truth is hard for us to grasp.

Also, if we've been schooled in theology or had a steady diet of spiritual "meat," we sometimes haven't the foggiest idea how to communicate with someone who is still on a "milk" diet. An immature Christian doesn't need laborious, complicated explanations stuffed with side comments.

If you are asked, "Why do you study the Bible?" or "Why do you believe Jesus is the only way?" do you find yourself answering with a lengthy treatise? Do you search your mind for the marvelous teachings you've received from a biblical scholar?

Instead of grabbing for things others have said, it would be far better to explain only what you personally know to be true...things you've experienced.

Whenever Jerry would ask me a simple question, I would give him a 20-point sermonette. I was a walking concordance, and it often prompted him to ask me for answers instead of searching for himself.

I'll never forget some of our "spiritual discussions." During a conversation after church one Sunday, I confronted him with "You know what your problem is? You just don't want to grow. That's it."

Jerry gripped the wheel tightly, his knuckles white. "That does it!" he said. "All you can think about is **grow, grow, grow.** You go to this meeting, you go to that meeting. But it seems to me that all that activity doesn't have a thing to do with salvation. There's only one thing you need and that is to accept what Christ has done on Calvary. Once you are saved, that's it. Nothing else is required."

While his point about salvation was true, the fact that

he criticized my emphasis on growth made me angry. I felt defensive, but this hardly seemed the time for an in-depth argument, so I let the matter drop. I was churning inside though. How dare he criticize my desire to grow spiritually? Growth is what makes the "abundant life" possible!

Many weeks later, while reading his Bible one evening, Jerry said something that sounded as if he might be having second thoughts.

"My faith isn't like yours," he said. "You always seem so sure and so strong. By comparison, I keep wondering if you're trying to tell me my faith isn't valid?"

I sat stunned. I was glad to hear him say something positive about my faith, but his beginning to question his own salvation made me shake in my boots. **Have I driven him to this?** I wondered. If it were true that I had shattered his faith by all my zealous campaigning, then I didn't have much to be proud of.

Jerry began to turn the pages of his Bible. "Here...I found this earlier." He began reading from Acts 1:8. "But you shall receive power when the Holy Spirit has come upon you..."

"Nyla," he said, "I don't see that power in my Christian life. Great things don't happen to me that prove unmistakably that I have the power of the Holy Spirit. And if I don't have the power of the Holy Spirit, doesn't that mean I'm not a true Christian?"

So Jerry really was questioning his salvation status. I found it hard to believe. Wasn't he the one who had answered the pastor so eloquently when asked, "If you should die tonight and God were to say to you, 'Why should I let you into My heaven?' what would you say?"

I remembered Jerry's answer: "It's only because of Jesus that I could enter. I'd never have enough righteousness or good deeds of my own to qualify for entrance. He paid the price by sacrificing His life so that I could enter."

With an answer like that, how could Jerry not be a believer?

Did Jerry have the Holy Spirit? He had to have had an initial encounter with the Holy Spirit in order to have said with conviction, "Jesus is Lord." (The Bible says that no man can say Jesus is Lord except by the power of God's Spirit.)

I think Jerry was having difficulty putting his finger on the role the Holy Spirit plays in causing believers to hunger after righteousness. Perhaps Jerry had experienced an initial infilling of the Holy Spirit, but had not experienced the power that comes with the fullness of the Spirit.

Another way to explain that is to compare marriage and salvation. For example, a couple is married the moment the wedding is complete. The reality of being married comes later, in the day-to-day living out of that commitment. A couple is no less married on the wedding day than on the 500th or 5,000th day. Marriage, then, is both an act and a process. It is somewhat the same with salvation.

Jerry didn't get his answer that evening. He wrestled for several months with the conflict between his desires to see power in his life and to rest in the claim, "I'm saved. That's all I need."

Nor was that the last of our moments of truth. I remember one which occurred as I was preparing to go to a women's meeting at the church.

"Nyla," Jerry said. "I don't understand your intense

desire to strive for spiritual gains. I'm not like that. I don't see why you think it is so necessary. Is it just a difference in our appetites, or is something wrong with me?"

I fumbled awkwardly for the right words. I tried to explain that in my life, being in love with Jesus was responsible for all this activity. I was like a bride who couldn't get enough of her groom. My response seemed to annoy Jerry. I could tell because his brow wrinkled and that steely-eyed look came my way again.

"Does my relationship with Jesus threaten you in some way?"

He paused as if it were a bonus question on a television game show. The air was heavy with awkwardness and expectation.

"Now that you mention it..." His eyes dropped and his speech became more subdued. "The more of Jesus you get, the less of you I get. Since you've fallen in love with Jesus, all I get are your left-overs."

That was it. Jerry didn't want to warm up to Jesus because Jesus was his competition. Jesus was "the other man in my life."

Why hadn't I seen it before? I had assumed that godliness and a God-first attitude would be an example that would make Jerry want the same for himself. How had things become so twisted and confused?

I started to cry. "Oh Jerry, I've messed things up so badly. I don't know what to say. I don't know how to talk to you about spiritual things without hurting you. I'm so ashamed."

He pulled me to himself. His arms were strong and warm. I sobbed until I thought my chest would cave in.

While I didn't see it at the time, God was answering the prayer I had uttered many months before..."God, lead Jerry and me to the place where we can approach You together." For the first time, I was on the same rung with him. We would climb together.

———————

Lord, how many times have I pushed my loved one away? Is my room so full of my religious paraphernalia that there's no room for my mate to find a place to rest or for us to share a laugh together? Have I set up so much "red tape" and so many requirements that my loved one thinks I've removed the welcome mat? Lord, keep me from these things. Amen.

CHAPTER 9

Up From the Pits

Being "in the pits" isn't the worst thing that can happen to you. Sometimes you learn more from your spiritual valley experiences than you do from the mountain-top.

In the months following my kitchen-sobbing, the wind was knocked out of my sails. I, a Spirit-filled believer, was in an embarrassing situation. Who wants to admit to marital unrest in a Christian family? Who wants to confess that one's self-willfulness is often bigger than the desire for God's will in marriage? Who wants to imagine an unbeliever peeking in the window and asking, "If that's the abundant life, why are there so many problems?"

One thing was certain—I didn't want to spend 30 or 40 more years like this. Somehow, I had to give my marriage all the strength and inspiration I could muster.

What was I to do? All my ploys had been worked and overworked. I asked myself, "If something is making matters worse, why continue it?" Since I didn't want religion to become a "no-no" at our house, I had to think of something.

Here are some of the changes that came about over the next few months and years. Nothing came quickly, but with persistence we could see glimmers of improvement.

I had to stop flaunting the importance of my religious activities. That was one of the first things and it was no easy task since I was in the throes of burning myself out in overcommitment to activities I thoroughly enjoyed. Since I was out sometimes three or four nights a week for church-sponsored functions, the cut-and-pare job was a monumental undertaking.

In my first book, **I Was an Overcommitted Christian,** I explained how Jerry and I learned to monitor and eliminate extraneous activities. If you suspect your daily schedule is getting in the way of effective witnessing to loved ones, you may find that book helpful.

I decided to see what would happen if I ceased my irksome verbal reminders of church activities. I told Jerry I was going to cut back on playing secretary for him. After all, what man, woman or child wants a mother-figure constantly reminding him or her to tie shoes, wipe noses, etc.? People get stronger when they take responsibility for their own doings.

Sure, they might forget a lot in the beginning, and they might drop an activity you think is important, but in the long run they'll be more committed to the things **they** choose. Maybe this idea will make you lose some sleep and gain some grey hair, but over the long haul, I believe the benefits are greater.

We re-instituted "date night." I needed to find more time alone with Jerry to rekindle our communication skills and our romance. So we re-instituted a practice we had let slip when the children were younger. What a treat! Sundays picked me up spiritually and "date night" lifted my emotional spirits. In the morning I'd wash my hair and give myself a fresh manicure. Later I'd put on something that I enjoyed wearing. When Jerry came home from work, we'd hire a sitter, and he and I would go window shopping or walking in the neighborhood. An hour's babysitting did wonders.

We decided to develop more activities that we could hold in common—both secular and religious. For too long we had been like ships that pass in the night, taking turns babysitting. We needed more ways to enhance our identity as a couple, so we took up ice-skating twice a week, began teaching a third-grade Sunday school class, and were in a play. And we did all these things together.

We concentrated on eliminating as much separation as possible on Sunday morning. Sundays usually had had us going in opposite directions once we got to church. Or I would leave Jerry standing in a hallway or foyer while I visited with a girl friend or made an important delivery that couldn't wait. You and your loved ones lose something when you're trying to conduct "business" on the Lord's day and in His house. Although it was hard, and sometimes inconvenient, I determined to deliver those things during the coming week. Most things I thought simply couldn't wait, could!

And I began saving those in-depth conversations until another time. If someone came to me with an issue that could mushroom into a lengthy discussion, I would say, "Give me a call this afternoon or first thing in the morning."

We've learned to make use of teachable moments by being available. How can you be sure others in your family feel needed and wanted, so they don't feel like outsiders? One of the ways we do it is by asking, "Have you had enough lovin' today?" I regularly ask the children and Jerry that question. I love the responses. Sometimes I get a quizzical look and then a warm little body cuddles up to me and says, "Mom, would you tickle my back?" While tickling, we exchange bits of information about the day's ups and downs.

Doors began to open when I first learned to make myself vulnerable. If you want someone to be open with you, you have to be open first. In our home I occasionally pose questions like, "Do you think I'm spending too much time at my typewriter? Do you feel pushed out of my life as a result of my activities? Am I going to too many meetings? Am I giving you enough of myself?"

If you don't react defensively to their responses, you'll find that others will initiate a few vulnerable questions of their own. Like, "Am I helping around the house enough? Am I getting home too late?"

In a nutshell, you need to create an environment that says, "It's safe to express ourselves as long as we are trying to be sensitive to the needs of others."

This skill doesn't develop overnight. It means you risk being "in the wrong" once in a while. You risk inconvenience. You risk abandoning hidden agendas.

Is it worth it? I predict your witnessing opportunities will double, your listeners will become receptive, and your effectiveness as an ambassador for Christ will flower, as you:

1. Build bridges, not roadblocks.

2. Learn to hear yourself as your listeners hear you.

3. Streamline your schedules so your loved ones won't feel pushed out by your commitments.

One additional suggestion: When non-church friends invite you to a ball game, concert or some other secular event, and you have a previous commitment at church, don't give a detailed excuse about why you cannot attend. Simply say, "I have a previous engagement, but I hope you'll ask me again."

If you find yourself always giving a "religious" reason for not being with friends outside your church, they may come to resent the church you want to interest them in and the Jesus they may find there. On the other hand, an occasional mention of something you're doing at church may pique their curiosity and make them a receptive audience. You need to find the balance.

Lord, I don't always sense when it is appropriate to talk about You. Sometimes I fill the air with important spiritual matters that only a few people care about. You know I love You more than anything, but guard me from projecting an image that suggests I have a rigid, one-track mind that has no room for anybody but You.

This week, help me to hear myself speak—to hear

myself as my listeners hear me.

Guard me from idle chatter. Remind me not to complain in front of unbelievers, since they might turn me off when I later try to tell them about a God who provides for every need.

Help me become a bridge-builder to You. Amen

CHAPTER 10

Are You Worth Listening To?

Nothing is more important in convincing a listener than credibility.

Situation 1: Tell me if you think the man described below would be considered credible by his secular friends.

Chuck graduated from a Christian high school, went to a Christian college and after graduation joined his father's insurance firm. From the first day on the job he was a "go-getter." He arrived early, stayed late and ate his lunch at his desk.

In the evening he returned to his apartment and settled down to a TV dinner, albums of Christian music and the challenge of finishing the Bible study he had started in the morning. Some evenings he went out to a young singles group meeting at his church. Other nights, weather and daylight permitting, he'd play softball with some of the guys from the church.

On Saturday mornings he'd go down to the church to see if he could help with the Sunday bulletin or perform fix-it jobs. On Sunday, he'd teach a young adult class, attend church, go to someone's house for dinner and then back to church in the evening for services.

Chuck had a subscription to the **New York Times,** but he seldom read it. His mother had bought him a subscription to **Newsweek** magazine but he never got beyond the pictures. On his nightstand were a couple of paperbacks, latest best sellers, but he just wasn't interested. He read Christian literature—daily Bible readings, a book of devotions and at least two Christian paperbacks each week. His radio played local religious music. Occasionally, however, he would switch to the news station, just so he'd know all was well in Washington and the world.

One evening someone from work invited him to supper, and he graciously accepted. They had arranged for a young lady to join them. During the meal someone brought up the subject of going to the beach on Sunday.

"Chuck, could you come?"

"Sorry," he answered, "I've got to teach a Sunday school class."

"Where do you go to church?" the young lady wanted to know.

"I go to the Fighting Faction Church. They really preach the Word over there." (Some fidgeting and clinking of silverware.) "Where do you go, Sue?"

"Well, I used to go to St. Anesthesia. That was before the minister left."

"Gee, Sue, you know you can't go to heaven unless you're born again. You can't be born again if you go to that church. Why don't you come to mine?"

Someone conveniently choked on a piece of meat and that was the end of the religious discussion.

I ask you: Do you think the Chucks of this world are going to be listened to with open ears?

It is important to make sure you can relate to others...especially if they aren't Christians. Be credible and people will listen.

Situation 2: Witnessing to people in your immediate family is especially demanding. Who else can infuriate so effectively? Who can challenge credibility more? You're in the furnace of testing when you try to teach a family member anything!

Once my father tried to teach my mother how to drive. What a disaster! It went something like this:

"Virginia...Virginia...you've got the key upside down. What's the matter with you?" A little later..."No, no, Virginia, you have to make the clutch depress completely. Stop! You'll strip the gears. All right, Virginia, cut the engine. I can't take this."

A few days later they tried again. This time Mother was able to get around the block, though with a lurching gait. She'd made it, but she'd also had it with free lessons. When she got inside the house, she plopped the keys on the kitchen table and with a quivering lower lip she said these memorable words: "I'd rather walk!"

I don't think Dad ever realized what was happening.

Truism number one about witnessing to our families: **We expect family members to be geniuses at learning and grasping new ideas.**

Truism number two: **All human beings have a tendency to comment only on the things others do wrong.** Failing to approve of what others do right places the speaker in a negative light and bystanders don't think he or she is worth listening to.

(I should add that Mother did learn to drive...no thanks to my dear father, bless his soul. If it hadn't been for the U-2 Can Learn To Drive School, she'd never have made it.)

To consider:

When was the last time you said something affirmative to a contrary member of your family?

Do you tend to comment only on negative behavior? For instance, do you mention table manners only when someone has spilled the milk?

To be worth listening to in your family, you have to be more positive than negative. So find something nice to say to that teenager who needs a haircut.

I heard author Karen Wise on television the other day. She's the author of **Confessions of a Totaled Woman**...don't you love that title? She said something that bears repeating: "What's important and what's insignificant?" Do you make everything sound important? Do you reprimand transgressions in toothbrush routine as strongly as you do missing a curfew?

Although her comments were directed to the training of children, I'm going to make an analogy to witnessing to family members. "First," she said, "I ask myself, 'Is what I'm dealing with violating a principle of God?' If not, then I'd better soft-pedal that issue so that when I have something really significant to say, my child will take notice and realize that **Mom is saying something important.**"

Now compare that to witnessing to family members. If you make a big deal out of every small transgression, then when you need to rally the forces of heaven behind you for something big, your family may completely miss God's message for them.

Truism number three: **Save up for the important messages.** That way you won't have laryngitis when they need to go forth.

Situation 3: This moving and beautiful story involves a witness outside the family. If you ever found yourself refereeing a family squabble, you could use this. It has universal application.

I had a friend in Calfornia whose father-in-law, Joe, was a retired minister. After 30-odd years in the pulpit he decided to take on something new; and since he discovered he was too vital and not yet crotchety or feeble enough to sit in a rocking chair all day, he decided to try his hand in the insurance business.

After a few months of learning the ropes, Joe found that making calls and helping people with their financial concerns was an ideal springboard for the subject of the best "life assurance" he'd ever found—Jesus.

One evening while this former pastor was going through a presentation with a young couple, his spiritual antennae picked up some disquieting vibrations. He boldly confronted the couple.

"Something isn't right with you two. You're having problems, aren't you?"

The couple (I'll call them John and Mary) looked at each other sheepishly.

"Yes," they admitted. There had been much strife in recent months. Unsure if they'd even be together a year from now, they were wondering why they were listening to a presentation on life insurance and beneficiary planning. Where would this unusual conversation lead?

The insurance salesman continued, "Excuse me. I've had experience in the area of family problems. I used to do a lot of counseling. Mind if I tell you something?"

Truism number four: **Don't barge into presentations. Ask permission to proceed, as Joe did. Then people are committed to listen.**

The two gave a perfunctory nod. They'd obligated themselves to whatever came next.

"I can tell you exactly what to do, and if you do it, I can guarantee results. Not many offers today promise that much. You want to hear it?" (Again, Joe was getting their permission to go on.)

"First thing you have to do is follow this recipe exactly as I give it. Second, you must do it every night for at least three nights. After the third night you'll start to see results. If you keep it up, there's no telling what miracles you'll see in your marriage." (He really had them eating out of his hand then.)

"Here's what you do, John. When you go to bed, tonight, you put your arms around Mary and say, 'Thank you, God, for Mary, **just as she is.'**"

John looked a little shocked. He was probably thinking, what if I don't feel like putting my arms around her? But Joe was one step ahead.

"I don't care if you don't feel like giving her a hug, do it anyway. And Mary? You do the same. You put your arms around John and you say, loud enough for both of you to hear it, 'Thank you, God, for John, **just as he is.'** If you do that for three days...well, you'll see."

Joe picked up his hat and started toward the door.

Then he turned and said, "Remember I guarantee results. Will you pick up the option and give it a try?" (In sales terminology, that's called "asking for the sale." It confronts the buyer with a verbal commitment.)

John and his wife agreed they had nothing to lose, so they promised they would do as he said. They didn't realize Joe was committed to them, too. He wasn't about to plant seeds and dash off without the knowledge that they were being watered. Joe was the kind of man who followed through with what he started.

"Be seeing you!" and Joe was gone.

A few days later he was back. "Hi, just finding out if my customers are happy with the recipe I left." The look on Mary's face told everything. A grin broke out from ear to ear.

"You know," she said, "I thought we were crazy to agree to such a simple thing. John and I used to go to church when we were first married but that slipped along with a lot of other things in recent years. Then you came along with your guarantee. Well, we did it.

"The first night it sounded so funny to hear ourselves saying 'thank you' to God. By the second night, it sounded a little easier and by the third night I found myself thinking about what the last part of the sentence really meant. 'Thank you, God, for John, just as he is.' I thought you should thank God only for the things you like; I never thought about thanking God for the imperfections and aggravations."

John then walked into the room. "Hi! Checking up on us, I see. Hey, I want to tell you something. When you told us to say that prayer, I would never have believed what could happen. Just hearing my voice saying, 'Thank you, God, for Mary, just as she is,' really tore me up. I felt I was committing myself all over again to our marriage."

What a story! If I hadn't known the daughter-in-law, I might never have believed such a thing could happen.

Is there someone you need to pray for, a person who needs to hear you say, "Thank you, God, for_____ just as he (she) is"? Stop and do it now. Don't read it. Say it out loud. You need to hear yourself say it. It will be the beginning point of setting you free! And it has the plus of putting your prayers right in the lap of God so He can pour His healing into your relationships.

————————

Dear Lord, please make me a more credible witness as I release forgiveness. With the release, my loved one becomes more acceptable. When the loved one feels acceptable, he is more open to the gospel and to Your love. When I say "just as he is" I am saying, "I forgive him for being as human as I am." When Your love binds us together, we'll be able to listen to each other. Thank You, Lord. Amen.

Section Three

GUIDELINES FOR ACTION

Checklist for a Credible Lifestyle

Food for Thought

CHAPTER 11

Checklist for a Credible Lifestyle

Try to get a general overview of your lifestyle. Are you aware that your weak spots are the first thing an unbeliever or spiritual skeptic will focus on?

Non-Christians look at the way Christians spend their time, energy and money. Then they consciously or subconsciously form conclusions.

Obviously, no one can be perfect this side of heaven. We're not perfect—we're forgiven. But others don't necessarily see that.

Suppose you spend most of your waking hours in religious activities, Bible studies, meetings or socials at church. Your unsaved family members, or your closest friends, begin to take note of how much of your attention is left over for them.

While God is the most important thing in your life, and well He should be, it is important for you to keep a finger in other activities to balance out the spiritual. Then, you see, your credibility is enhanced because your loved one is convinced you can relate to his interests as well as your own.

While others may not share my view, I have wondered in recent years whether the Jonestown massacre and the Jim Jones People's Temple cult evolved into a bizarre state of blind worship because of overinvolvement and skewed interests. When I see any famous personality taking extreme positions or living an extreme lifestyle I ask the question, "Is the rest of his life in balance with

the religious aspects?" I could be wrong, but I think **balance is the key.** Balance protects one's sanity and one's health.

I've discovered that balance is essential in my personal life as well. A number of years ago when it seemed I was spending all my time in only one area, I became about 13 pounds overweight. If you've ever seen me, you know I'm not what you'd call a big person.

To add 13 pounds to a 5'2" frame meant I became a sleepyhead. Too tired to clean the house, too tired to exercise, too tired...period. Not fat, mind you, just tired most of the time. Neither Jerry nor I had ever engaged in a regular program of exercise. Both of us were slowly approaching those "middle-age-spread" years so we decided it was time to take action.

We began to take ice-skating lessons. Not only did we get exercise, we were guaranteed of having at least one or two nights each week as "date nights." Our bodies firmed up and so did our relationship. We've been doing that for seven years. Now that we've seen the advantage exercise has been to our lives, we have observed that the time spent in religious activities is also more relaxed and less intense. We're enjoying everything more.

Witnessing opportunities have come out of that skating experience. One fellow skater had grown up in a Jewish home, but had never stayed close to the Hebrew faith. We had invited him to share an Easter dinner with us. Simon (I'll call him) knew bits and pieces about Christian beliefs. He was open to our hospitality, even for Christian holidays. If we played Christian music, we played it softly and usually chose something that sounded Yiddish.

Occasionally the subject of religion would come into the conversation. Over the years, I noticed Simon's thought pattern and logic didn't follow that of the Western hemisphere. It seemed alien...almost mystically Eastern. Given the same facts that might appear in a gospel presentation, Simon would come to a completely different conclusion.

When I spoke with Simon about religious things, it became obvious to me that I didn't have answers he could understand. I tried. But something was lost in the translation from my spoken intent to his listening. Still, I didn't despair.

A couple of years ago something interesting happened. As Simon watched Jerry and me, I believe that, in spite of our inability to articulate our faith convincingly, the Lord began working in his life.

One evening during a skating session, Simon came over to the side of the rink where Jerry and I were standing.

"Hey, Nyla...tell me something. How come you've got such a glow?" His eyes darted in Jerry's direction and he pointed at him. "He's got it too."

I smiled. No words. Just smiled. I don't think it was shyness that prevented me from speaking.

"Is it the vitamins you and Jerry take?" he wanted to know.

"No," I said. And I said no more.

"Is it because you're happily married?"

This time I shrugged. "Well, partly, but that's not really it."

Simon looked intently at us for a long time. Then he leaned forward and whispered in my ear. "I know, it's **Jesus Christ,** isn't it?"

Who do you think told him that? I wish I could say the conversation that ensued convinced him to get on his knees on that very spot and ask Jesus to become his Messiah. It didn't.

In fact, Simon told me that evening he'd received a letter from a friend in the mail. This friend had recently had a conversion experience and was totally elated. In her letter she quoted Old Testament passages and New Testament verses. Simon was grossly offended. He said to me, "I was insulted by her letter. It was as if she didn't think I knew the Bible. I've read the Old Testament and even parts of the New."

At that moment I knew that the usual presentation would not suffice with Simon. He was different.

"Simon," I said, "tell me what offended you most about the Christian testimony she tried to give you—so I won't do that to you." (I didn't want to come across as defensive. I knew I needed to keep the doors open.) I listened as Simon told me the things that turned him off. It placed me in a vulnerable, rather than a defensive, position, and that, I figured, was what the situation called for.

To my knowledge, Simon is no longer skating. He's divorced and has taken up Zen Buddhism. I wrote him in my last Christmas letter, "When you're finished with Zen, I hope you'll ask yourself again, what is it that makes Jerry's and Nyla's lifestyle so complete? Remember the answer you gave us so long ago, from your very own lips? 'Is it Jesus Christ?'"

Someday I believe Simon, the Jew, will know the Messiah. He's had a model and an example and a quiet "soft-sell" gospel presentation. We've done everything possible to keep the doors open.

If you suspect any part of your life might be out of balance, I encourage you now to pick up a pencil and complete the following questionnaire. If it helps you develop a more balanced life, you may be further ahead in the race, in terms of winning people to Christ.

One thing more: A balanced life will give you more "miles per spiritual gallon." You won't burn out and you'll have more of yourself to share for the gospel's sake over the long haul. (You do want to be around for the long haul, don't you?)

First, let's obtain a general overview. On the first part of the questionnaire, check the "yes" column if you are strong in the area mentioned (80% or more). If, however, you are weak in that area, or it is non-existent in your life, check the "no" column.

Yes No

1. My eating habits: Am I getting good nutrition?
2. Rest: Do I get plenty of sleep?
3. Spiritual feeding: Am I regularly able to hear good sermons, attend Bible studies, etc.?
4. Social: Do I enjoy times of fellowship and companionship?
5. Physical exercise: Do I take fairly vigorous exercise at least two hours a week?
6. Intellectual stimulation: Do the things I read or watch on TV cause me to grow in my appreciation of the arts, politics, music, world events, etc.?
7. Vacations: Do I take one faithfully every year?
8. Passive reflection time: Do I take time to rest? Time for "do nothing" solitude? Time for reflection?
9. Quiet time: Do I have a set time for daily devotions or personal Bible study?

How did you do? I hope you had lots of "yes" answers. If you were not able to answer "yes" for the last item, I should alert you right away: You're on shaky ground. A "yes" for the last one is a rock of safety God has provided for you. You need it more than you need any of the others. Start your day with it. Don't wait until you go to bed at night. At the breakfast table or while you're still in bed with a cup of hot coffee, your Bible will give you something to remember all day. You'll see a difference between morning devotions and those at night (if you have to make a choice).

If you don't know how to have a quiet time, I suggest you go to your local Christian bookstore and ask to see their devotional materials.

The next thing you need to do is take a closer look at

your weekly activities.

List the major responsibilities you have outside of your family and occupation (work, or domestic duties if you're a full-time homemaker).

_____

_____

_____

NOTE: If you need more space, you're probably overcommitted!

Again check the appropriate column:

Yes No

—   —   1. Outside of Sunday morning worship, do you attend more than three church-related or Bible- centered activities?

—   —   2. Are most of your activities in the service or "doing" category?

—   —   3. Are most of your activities "refueling" or edifying rather than service oriented? More Bible studies than visiting the sick, etc.

—   —   4. Are you gone from home more than two nights per week on an average? If yes, list below those meetings, outings, sports, obligations, etc.

_____

_____

_____

_____

_____

—   —   5. Do you find, with all your activities, you have a tendency to substitute some other church-sponsored Bible-centered activity for private Bible study? (God does desire daily time **alone** with you!)

— — 6. Do you find you have difficulty saying "no" to worthy causes...and then later do a poor job because you're not committed to the task?

— — 7. Is your family complaining that your activities are taking you away from them too much of the time? (God gave you a family to help keep you stable and balanced. They're worth listening to, no matter how important you think your commitments are.)

— — 8. Do you have so many commitments that your personal grooming is going to pot?

— — 9. Do you find you are servng on committees, etc., for which you do not have the interest or the talent?

— — 10. Are you beginning to have more physical problems: flu, virus, colds, etc.? (Often this is the body's first signal that you are abusing the "temple" which God has said each believer's body is.)

— — 11. Are you beginning to show nervous or emotional stress? Unusually fast speech, inability to concentrate during conversations, inability to carry a conversation through to its logical end?

— — 12. Are you short-tempered with your loved ones?

— — 13. Are you having difficulty falling asleep at night?

— — 14. Are you persistently short-tempered with associates and family? (You could be overworked and out of balance.)

— — 15. If you have children, have you noticed, since you've added additional responsibilities or commitments, they are experiencing more problems in school, relationships with others, etc.?

— —   16. Is your marriage suffering under the strain of added commitments?

— —   17. If your spouse is not a Christian, does he (she) feel threatened by the attention you are giving to your religious pursuits?

— —   18. Are you daydreaming more than usual?

— —   19. Are others avoiding you? (You may be too intense.)

— —   20. Does your spouse constantly take second place in your life to your activities at church?

— —   21. Has at least 80% of your activities become non-family and centered at the church? (If you're a minister, obviously this is a tough one to change. But if your family is complaining in loud tones of discontent, maybe you should consider the priestly life of Eli, in the Old Testament. He had no time for his sons because of church involvement. And you know how wicked they became!

— —   22. How easily can you unwind? When it is time to relax, do you find your mind is still rehashing business, current events, or your golf score? NOTE: Try something so unrelated to your work that you have no choice but to relax: soak in a hot tub, run around the block, etc.

Now, look over your answers. Do you have more "yes" than "no" responses? Ouch!

Ask someone close to you to look over your list of responsibilities at the beginning of the questionnaire. When they counsel you concerning jobs that could be delegated, watch out. Your first reaction may be a defensive, "I can't **possibly** give that one up."

When you are out of balance, you are not in a good position to judge your lifestyle. You're overloaded and running on borrowed energy. If you don't stop now, you'll have to pay a bigger price later...maybe even a tragic price. Listen to your friends.

Do you know why we become overcommitted and overburdened? We get so caught up in the "I have to's" that we can't see when we need to have someone help us. We're so proud! If only we could be like Moses. He knew he couldn't hold Amalek and his army back unless he continued to hold up his rod. When he grew weary and couldn't hold the rod forth, the Amalekites gained on the Israelites. It was only when Moses allowed Aaron and Hur to hold his hands up for him that he was able to prevail.

Friend, you're not Super-Christian. You're only one person among many. God is so great and sovereign that if you can't do a job, He'll either call on someone else or put it on hold.

"But they need me! If I don't do this job, everything will fold," you insist.

Wait a minute! Do you think more of yourself than you should? Remember, Romans 12:3 says, "I bid everyone among you not to think of himself more highly than he ought" (RSV).

The most important thing right now is not that you finish every task or complete every project. The most important thing is to ask yourself, "Am I conserving my life's energy in such a way that I'll be around to finish the last mile?"

It is vital that you not only have credible words coming out of your mouth; you need a credible lifestyle to back them up.

———————

Lord, I confess that my lifestyle needs changing. I've become so caught up in getting the gospel out that I've neglected some other things. I want to sit quietly now, alone with You, Lord. Give me guidance in what changes to make. I want Your help. Amen.

CHAPTER 12

Food for Thought

I've learned a great deal about serving up Christianity in a palatable form. Oddly enough, I learned some of my most valuable lessons from observing the food habits of my children.

Kids, it seems, will eat anything else before they accept a bubbling lasagna or spicy beef bourguignon. Woe to the parent who tries to introduce anything new beyond pizza, hamburger or super-shake. It's a losing battle. There are days when I want to say, "I resign. I quit."

We look at those we love, those with whom we want so much to share Jesus, with an eye to what they're taking in to feed their spirits, and often we see things like pornography, drugs, X-rated movies, double-standard morality and situation ethics, just to mention a few.

In many cases, our loved ones are not bad people. They're good people—they do nice things for others. But they're missing the glue that holds it all together: Jesus Christ. Neither a diet critically low in spiritually redeeming nutrients nor one which is a bare subsistence regimen can support life.

It has taken more than 10 years for me to figure out how to get our children to eat well. And it is taking at least 30 to determine how to feed people spiritually.

Let me share some principles you may find helpful in both areas.

1. **Get their permission before you try something new.** No sneaking crushed carrots into puddings. It's dishonest. Tell your kids there's something new in there...let 'em guess. With each taste, you're one step closer.

In witnessing, don't assume it's necessary to trick loved ones to get them to come to a church function. Be honest and aboveboard. For example: "There's a movie being shown at church tonight on parenting. I'd like to see it. Would you like to come with me?"

2. **If you find something they like, don't serve it 10 days in a row.** I used to be desperate, but you'd be better off serving the vegetable only once a week at the beginning.

In witnessing, if a friend or loved one expresses interest in the Sunday morning services, you should avoid the implication that you expect them to continue going regularly with you. **Never assume.**

If the person is a new Christian, he will have a hard time establishing new patterns. His church attendance may be erratic in the beginning. If he misses a Sunday, whatever you do, don't imply that he's lost his new-found salvation and might be returning to a life of ruin! Be gentle.

You might want to share that, in your own life, you have difficulty adopting new practices. (Doing daily exercises, remembering to take medicine, etc.) You could say, "I know I'll be better off if I do those things, but it sure is hard." Then leave the subject. Don't start reciting any list, for example: "Well, Charlie, if you're going to be a **good** Christian, you've got to worship every Sunday, come to prayer meeting on Wednesdays, quit swearing and stop chewing that awful tobacco."

Suppose the person says, "I don't want to go to church again this Sunday." Don't give up. Ask again another time. And when the person rejects your offer, whatever you do, don't reflect disappointment. It implies a judgmental attitude on your part. Instead, give that person the biggest smile you can muster and say, "That's okay. Maybe another time." Then change the subject. No lectures. And then you pray silently, "God, let there be another opening, another day. Let me recognize the time **of Your choosing** for further conversations about worship."

3. **Don't serve six-course meals for starters. One thing at a time, in the beginning...later you can bring on the variety.**

When I first started giving our babies "jar food," I used to line up the jars, and serve one kind for a few days. Once the baby demonstrated that the new food would not cause a rash or sudden regurgitation, I'd proceed to a new food, and later add others, one by one, fruits, cereals, vegetables, and the meat.

If a person is a new believer, you can easily overload his system by giving him too many things in the beginning. Only rarely is there a spiritual diner who can handle a smorgasbord right away.

Start with **one** thing. If that sits well, suggest another meeting or study or social event.

We do a disservice to new believers if we give them too much too soon. They may want to please us, and jump at a chance to do everything we suggest. **You are responsible to help them develop good eating habits from the start. Don't encourage them to neglect good stewardship of time and energy.**

When I was little, they tell me, I used to eat a plate of food starting with one thing and proceeding to the others **only** after each item had been completely finished. My mother told me repeatedly, "Nyla, food tastes so much better when it is mixed. The variety really improves it."

Well, I resisted. Years went by before I could bring myself to try it her way. She was right. Food does taste better that way. We both learned that babies don't do anything until they're ready.

Spiritual babies may be that way too. For years they

may be content to attend only worship services. Many of us motherly types cajole them into trying more activities at church, but they balk. They're still babies and they're trying to tell us that. How we need to listen!

Sometimes it will be possible to gently suggest that further down the track, they shouldn't be surprised if they start getting interested in more activities, maybe Bible study and prayer. It's a natural progression. Given positive encouragement, they'll come along in time. But don't be surprised if it takes years.

4. **Don't start with the meat courses.** Babies' systems can't take heavy proteins in the beginning. Meat, for a child, is an acquired taste and as he grows older, he learns that a hamburger is ultimately more satisfying than buttered broccoli, and will head for the hamburger first!

Apply that principle in the spiritual realm. When you take a new believer to a Bible study or prayer group, the experience may be too "meaty" or overwhelming, and you might get a reaction like this: "I felt so conspicuous. I was afraid someone would ask me to quote a Bible verse like some of the others were doing. But I still have trouble finding the book of Luke."

What should you do? You might want to consider that those groups appear too threatening, even though they satisfy your desire for spiritual meat perfectly. You could suggest events which are more social in nature or lecture-oriented.

5. **If, after repeatedly introducing foods that are good for them, they still tell you "no...absolutely no!" you have no other choice—change the menu.**

This is the toughest part of feeding. With real babies, or with spiritual babies, you may have to search the cupboard for something they will finally eat. You could find yourself exploring foods you never would have chosen as palatable. If your loved one needs a liturgical setting to feel close to God, while you prefer a less formal service, you may need to compromise.

But don't compromise on the major tenets of the faith. Would the change to a new church mean you'd have to abandon belief in Jesus as God the Son, equal with the Father? Would you have to disavow the inspired nature of Scripture?

Would a change in churches require you to deny that Jesus is the only sacrifice possible to reunite us with the Father? **Major on the majors, and minor on the minors.** If it's merely music or the form of worship that is holding you back—those are minors, not majors.

Love often makes sacrifices, but never at the price of losing fellowship with Christ.

I've known husbands and wives who have been willing to give up a tenacious grasp on denominational loyalties, and having done so without compromising the gospel message have found they still were able to be fed in new surroundings.

6. **Do I want my loved ones' appetites satisfied on my terms or God's? Do I insist that others like the same food as I?** (Nothing shuts doors more quickly.)

Never say around a child, "How can you stand peas? Yuck—peas!" When you see someone making a mustard sandwich, stifle the commentary. Refrain from a grimace! (Children should give parents the same courtesy, but they don't seem able to do that until they start inviting dates home for supper.)

In the spiritual sense, avoid saying things like, "Margaret, how can you stand going to a church like that? It's so stiff and formal."

If someone tells you he loves Bach, don't counter with, "My dear, it's contemporary Christian music or nothing."

If a friend says, "I like to worship with my hands up," don't deflate him with, "Hands up? I think folded hands are better." The Bible recognizes a very wide spectrum for worship postures.

There are as many tastes and preferences in worship as there are different people. Your way and mine are not the only ones that count.

———————

Lord, we know this is how the world will recognize Your disciples—by the way we love one another. Help me do it with more than glib, gushy phrases. May we put our life on the line—and truly love people to Jesus. Amen.

Section Four

PRAYER POWER UNLEASHED

Prayer Pointers

Prayer Petitions

Prayer Partner

Can You Pray With Your Loved One?

Pawnshop Prayer Box

Do You Have a "10"?

How Can I Know If I'm the One to Witness?

CHAPTER 13

Prayer Pointers

Here are some Bible verses and practical suggestions to help you keep your lines clear so that prayer power can flow. If you've been praying for months, and even years, for something and haven't seen a glimmer of an answer, some of these ideas may help you spot the problem.

1. **Approach God early.** Don't wait until the problem gets so big that its tentacles are choking your voice box. "Oh God, thou art my God; early will I seek thee; my soul thirsteth for thee, my flesh longeth for thee in a dry and thirsty land, where no water is" (Psalm 63:1, KJV).

2. **Approach God's throne with confidence.** As you read your Bible, underline phrases that appear as promises to God's people. Copy these promises and put them beside your phone or near the sink or your mirror. Let them remind you of God's intentions toward you.

When you stake your claim on a particular verse, though, don't make the mistake of saying to God, "It says here in Your Word that this should happen, so I insist that you do it!" Humbly request, but never command. The Bible says we can cry aloud and God will hear us. But the cry of a haughty child with a clenched fist demanding rights and privileges is an irritation to our heavenly Father.

God may not give you everything you ask for, but He will give you what's good for you. So the next time you're tempted to think His answer was slipshod or half-hearted, look again. He doesn't arrange all the chess pieces and shout, "Checkmate," in one move.

Praise Him for all the advances and retreats, and don't get impatient and leave before the end of the game. Stick around. Be persistent in prayer. Believe He is working out the answers according to **His** purpose, not yours (Luke 18:1-8; Matthew 7:7-11; Mark 11:24).

3. **Approach God with clean hands.** If you've got resentments or grudges (against God or anyone), confess them right away. Get the air cleared. For example, pray, "I've been angry with myself, and You, God, because it's taking so long to see anything positive happening. I've nursed ill feelings about words said to me. It gets in the way of praying for my loved one.

"I know that You, Lord, already know my heart and the darkness that often hides there. Turn Your cleansing light on this and burn away the impurities right now so my prayers won't be hindered." There! Now you have access to God's ear. Now you can crawl into His lap and be conforted by the warmth of His arms.

4. **Run a quick check on the content of your prayers.** Do they consist mostly of "Give me this or that"? Or do you always have a few words of praise for God at the beginning? Something that reflects adoration? Something that reflects confession? Something that reflects giving thanks for all He's done for you?

Then, do you **end** with your prayer request list? (An easy way to remember the ingredients of prayer is to think of the acrostic, ACTS: Adoration, Confession, Thanksgiving, Supplication.)

Just think! God may have allowed a certain situation to exist so that you will develop a stronger prayer life. You might as well get in training. You could be in a fight for someone's soul for years to come.

God doesn't make any mistake when He lets you wait it out. He knows exactly what He's doing. Someone once explained this phenomenon to my satisfaction: "You're watching the parade through a knot-hole in the fence. God has the vista-vision from beginning to end."

Father, I need to use our prayer time better. I frequently plead for Your wisdom in accomplishing something and the next minute want to rush You into a quick answer. Forgive me. I want to give You honor. Amen.

CHAPTER 14

Prayer Petitions—Telling God How to Work

I remember attending a certain women's meeting a number of years ago. Two women in the group had been at odds with each other for months. The issues seemed petty to the rest of us and we were painfully aware that neither woman was willing to shelve differences.

One evening, an open confrontation surfaced during a crucial planning session. The chairman decided to stop further discussion by suggesting we pray for unity.

A few of us prayed short sentence-prayers. Then one of the offending women began to pray. "God, make Mary see that she is wrong in her thinking. Make her realize she is tearing the group into factions when she persists in holding her views...as unscriptural as they are!" Ouch! Even in prayer they were at each other's throats.

What was happening? One woman was trying to manipulate the relationship even while she was praying...passing judgment, trying to shame her opponent into submission, into her way of thinking.

Have you ever tried to manipulate another person's behavior under the guise of prayer?

I recall hearing a friend tell me of the mealtime prayers of her five-year-old: "God, show Daddy he's wrong and make him give me back my allowance."

Venomous judgments can pour forth in prayer—unless we realize its true purpose. Prayer is not a manipulative tool to get what you want out of God or others.

Let's get down to the specifics of prayer. How do you pray for someone you love? Husband? Wife? Child? Boyfriend? Girl friend?

Initially you probably have used the petition, "Get John saved." Later, as impatience grows, you change that slightly to, "God, save John by Christmas." Then, as opportunities seem promising and imminent, you alter the prayer to "God, save John this Friday at the prayer meeting."

Though we are urged to pray for specifics, couldn't that be interpreted as telling God how to do His job?

Why not, instead of praying that your loved one will get spiritually "zapped," focus on something that must precede that end product? Start smaller. Visualize the person as hungry to know God.

If you're having trouble doing that, stop and say a prayer for yourself, "Lord, I don't seem to have enough faith for this. I can't visualize _____(name)_____ as hungry for You. Lead me to the place in my spiritual growth where I can believe it is possible."

You can't pray well for things you have trouble believing. Ask yourself if your prayer is too big or too general, and focus on something smaller.

Another idea is to formulate prayers that are short-ranged and measurable. For example, if you were to pray to lose 50 pounds, that prayer might be too big. Instead pray for the smallest unit of time close to you: today. "Lord, help me to experience control of just **one** eating urge today. Just one." That request is both short-term and measurable. You'll know when you have an answer, and over a period of weeks, if you continue that prayer, you will notice a difference!

Transfer that application to a personal situation. "Lord, give me one moment today in which I can love my wife or husband with a word or a touch...something that comes from you." That's short term and that's measurable, and it gets at the heart of your wife's (husband's) desire to experience love. How do you expect her (him) to be able to recognize God's love unless she (he) has experienced love in a human way first?

If there is a prayer group you can join, that helps, too. But if you do that, here is a caution:

Don't divulge confidential matters about the person for whom you are praying. Ask yourself, "Would I want this prayer openly requested for me?" Some things should not be aired publicly. If there are deep things that must be said, confide in your pastor or that special prayer partner whom you can trust.

Also, a word about motives in praying. **It is possible to pray for the right thing with the wrong motive.**

Let me illustrate. I overheard a conversation in which two persons had approached a minister after a prayer meeting.

"Pastor," said one, "will you please pray for my husband? Will you pray that he'll become a believer?"

The pastor scratched his chin, and then asked a simple question. "Why do you want your husband to become a Christian?"

The lady looked shocked and slightly surprised by his query. "Well," she said, "you can't imagine how much it would mean to me to have my husband beside me in church on Sundays."

The pastor turned to the other woman standing nearby. He knew this person had had the same prayer desire for years. He asked the same question of her.

"Betty, why do you want your husband to become a believer?"

Her reply came in hushed tones. I noticed her eyes drop to the floor as she answered. "Because," she said, "I want him to know the love of God and not be afraid to die."

Someone could ask that same question of you. Be honest. What would be your first thought? Having a complete family in the pew on Sundays? Not having to go to church suppers with excuses for a teenager's absence? No longer having to worry about covering up for a wife, husband or relative with a drinking problem?

You've heard the answers given by the two wives and you may have been inclined in the past to adopt the first response as your own. Please, I ask you, if there is any question in your mind about your motives, stop and add this prayer to your daily petitions:

Lord, I think I might be wanting the conversion of ___(name)___ for the wrong reasons...perhaps more for my convenience and happiness. I ask You to plant in me, this very day, the desire to want my loved one whole and complete for far nobler reasons than the ones I've had before. Do for me what you did for David when he prayed..."Create in me a clean heart and renew a right spirit within me." Amen.

CHAPTER 15

Prayer Partner

If you've never had a prayer partner, you've missed something. A compatible, trustworthy and reverent fellow-believer as a prayer partner is a treasure beyond value.

It will immeasurably help in developing your prayer life if you can find someone who will admonish you with a mature hand, someone whose personal spiritual strengths stem from a close abiding daily walk with God. If you are an exuberant person, you might acquire more balance by seeking out someone who is more conservative, maybe a very quiet prayer warrior. If you're a young person, look for an older Christian.

Find a partner who has strengths that complement your weaknesses, and vice versa. If you have a prayer partner like that, you're potentially a hundred times stronger spiritually.

How do you locate such a person? Many years ago I found my first prayer partner by praying for one. I belonged to a Bible study group in California that was beginning a "2-3-Club." The "2-3" comes from the Bible verse that says, "Where two or three are gathered together in my name, there am I in the midst of them" (Matthew 18:20, KJV).

We were instructed to pray for one week before asking anyone to be our partner. It was a beautiful experience to see how God would impress our minds with the person of His choosing. In fact, there was a divine orderliness about the whole thing, and we did not have a number of people rushing to the same popular person. One by one, each of us found her own God-chosen prayer partner.

Some of us had never done this sort of thing before, so we needed a little help to get started. We didn't have an elaborate program, and many of us had never prayed aloud with another person. (Praying aloud was not one of the requirements.)

First we agreed to phone our partner at least once a week. Many women planned a certain day and time to make their call. We kept small notebooks and divided the pages into three columns. The first column was for the date of the prayer request, the second for the writing of the request, and the third for the date answered.

Having a prayer partner is one of the ways God can build our faith while releasing additional prayer power. We all took seriously the promise in Matthew 18:19, "Again I say unto you, that if two of you shall agree on earth as touching any thing that they shall ask, it shall be done for them of my Father which is in heaven" (KJV).

Whenever one of us had a need, we both would search our concordances to find a Bible verse to accompany the request, just to be sure we weren't asking amiss. We wanted to know if Bible-day believers had asked for the same things we were asking. Psalms and Proverbs proved to be among the favorite books for our Scripture searches.

When one had a need for faith for ourselves or a loved one, we looked in our concordances under the word "faith." We discovered that the disciples once asked Jesus to increase their faith and so it gave us the boldness to ask the Lord for the same thing. We found different kinds of faith: saving (Romans 10:9,10), temporary (Luke 8:13), intellectual (James 2:19) and dead faith (James 2:17,20). That helped us focus on our own specific needs as well as the needs of our loved ones.

Gradually, we became more skilled in wording our

prayer requests. Instead of saying, "Here's my prayer request—now agree with me," we would say, "Have I included everything I should? Should I leave anything out?" In the beginning, Linda, my partner, and I discovered we were often telling God how to run His business! We were inexperienced; God was very forgiving.

Sometimes if we had a nebulous concern, one we couldn't quite put into words, we'd say, "I've got a P.F.M. (pray for me) prayer." That was a "no-questions-asked" prayer. Sometimes the pain of a hurt was something we didn't want to verbalize, or maybe we couldn't quite bring ourselves to confess something. Without saying any more, we trusted the Holy Spirit to give our prayer partner the correct words and theme.

> "Likewise the Spirit also helpeth our infirmities, for we know not what we should pray for as we ought; but the Spirit itself maketh intercession for us with groanings which cannot be uttered. And He that searcheth the hearts knoweth what is the mind of the Spirit, because He maketh intercession for the saints according to the will of God" (Romans 8:26,27 KJV).

What an exciting year that was: Linda and I, our notebooks, Bibles and pencils, the many entries in the "answered" columns.

Best of all, I knew that God truly planned well when He ordained the fellowship of believers as a tool for uniting earthly hearts with a heavenly purpose.

Do you want a prayer partner? Pray about it for several days and then approach the person God puts on your heart. The two of you will become an invincible combination—your own "2-3-Club!"

CHAPTER 16

Can You Pray
With Your Loved One?

I'm sure some of you have already started the head-shaking. "Not me...not him! I'd be too embarrassed to pray with a loved one, and he'd never stand for it," you say.

Let's look at some situations in which you might be able to accomplish this. Sometimes God opens a door ever so slightly, and if you recognize the opportunity and can put aside your stage fright, you can pray without embarrassing the other person.

Perhaps your situation is so difficult at the present moment that you can't see how God could possibly alter circumstances to allow you to pray. Then ask Him to do just that! Be bold. Ask for the miracle you need to create the opportunity for prayer.

You may be thinking, "But I can't pray aloud. I've never done it before." That won't stop God. And besides, God will lead you carefully in little steps along the way. He can be very gentle.

Let me tell you how I learned. One day while driving my husband to work, I casually asked, "Jerry, what are your most pressing needs these days?" I didn't tell him what I was doing. He told me, and I kept that list mentally in my mind so I could pray during the day.

The next step: A few days later I asked Jerry the same question. This time when he told me, I offered a little more explanation. "I think I'll pray about those things."

I didn't know what Jerry would think of that. I figured

at the least he might humor me and say, "If that's what you want to do, go ahead."

Jerry was silent. He didn't say a word. I might have then proclaimed boldly, "Let's pray for them right now!" but I was a coward so I took it more slowly. I was satisfied with my simple declaration of intent.

I dropped Jerry off and started home with the children, who were then ages four and six. I knew I had to force myself to pray out loud as the next step in courage-building; mental prayers would not help me develop strong prayer legs. Besides, I needed to get used to hearing the sound of my voice. (This is a natural and necessary step toward eliminating a feeling of awkwardness when praying aloud with others.)

So, there in the car, I heard myself say, "God, Jerry is worried about deadlines. He's worried about having the right materials to fill orders. Show him You care about those things." It was easy for me to pray in front of the children. They didn't mind a few "ahs" and "ums" as I stumbled along.

About 5:00 o'clock that afternoon I received a call from a breathless, excited Jerry. "Nyla, you should do that more often. I'm seeing a difference here at work already. I can hardly believe it."

Jerry went on to relate that some obscure details had surfaced "almost miraculously" and it looked as if they would be able to complete some necessary transactions in time for the close of the fiscal year.

God knew I needed a "faith booster," and this was it. Jerry had been saying for months that he couldn't figure out how God could ever get involved in his business life. Now he was going to get a taste of divine involvement while I got an appetizer of answered prayer. That faith boost gave me the courage to ask Jerry the same question over and over, "What are your prayer needs today?"

I was getting stronger and bolder in my prayer life. I could feel the strength welling up inside me. So one day, as we were driving along, I posed my regular question and then I took a good grip on the wheel and said quickly, "Show Jerry that you're involved in his day, Lord. Amen." (And I didn't even close my eyes to pray!)

I didn't look over to see Jerry's reaction in the seat next to me, but I think he was pleased and touched. For sharing something in a spiritual sense, this sure beat the tense verbal scrimmages we used to have over religious topics. We were making progress.

I have to tell you that I was embarrassed to pray aloud like that. I could speak before audiences of hundreds, but praying in front of my husband was the hardest thing I had ever done.

You know what gave me the final push to do it? I began thinking, "Nyla, put your action where your mouth is. Don't just say you're going to do something; do it." I also remembered a Bible verse that instructs us not to withhold good from someone when it is in our power to do good. So I forged ahead.

When the fiscal year finally ended, the surprises and blessings were funneling into Jerry's life, pressed down and running over.

The day they closed the books, I picked Jerry up at work. For a man who is usually self-controlled, he was a river of words.

"I can hardly believe it," he said. "You know those prayer requests you've been working on for the past few months? Well, today I saw six of them come together in a matter of three hours. The only word to describe it is 'divine coincidence.'"

He talked animatedly all the way home. We pulled into the driveway, got out of the car and headed up the flagstone steps. It was fall and the wind was blowing leaves across our path as we climbed. Suddenly, Jerry reached out and grabbed one of my hands. Then he turned me to face him. Holding both my hands in his, he bowed his head.

"Thank you, Father, for answering prayers in such

obvious ways. I didn't realize You cared so much."

He let go of my hands and bounded up the steps with an air that suggested praying in the front yard was the absolutely normal thing to do.

My explanation for this unexpected, sudden spontaneity? Nothing except an overwhelming sense of awe and thankfulness that couldn't wait for church services the next Sunday. Jerry had decided it had to be done right then, so he did it. As I watched him unlock the door, I realized something else had been unlocked that day, too.

If it hadn't been for a California couple, Peggy and Dick Moe, we might never have become a family that prayed together. Although I'd yearned to have family devotions for years, I didn't know how to go about it. And as my religious suggestions had never met with much fanfare, I decided I'd have to be content with wishful thinking.

Once Jerry mentioned the possibility of having devotions. It was after a guest preacher spoke on family times together. But nothing happened.

You may think I had it easy, especially since my husband attended church. But let me tell you, it is often easier to rout the unsaved than to get Christians to do what they ought to be doing. Sure, we knew we "ought to" have devotions as a family, just as Christians know they "ought to" read their Bibles every day.

Did you know that only one out of ten professing Christians reads the Bible and prays at least ten minutes a day? Churchgoers have many of the same problems of inertia that the stay-at-homers have!

Back to Peggy and Dick Moe. They had no idea I'd been praying that God would open a door so we could have family devotions. You can imagine my surprise when one evening after our first dinner with the Moes, Dick said, "Would you like to join us in the living room for dessert and later some family devotions?" How easy he made it sound; I could never have carried that off with the same degree of casualness.

After dessert, Dick passed out Bibles and he asked Jerry to read a portion of Scripture. Then Dick read out of **Little Visits With God,** a children's devotional, and he ended with the few discussion questions listed at the end of the lesson. To our surprise, our five-year-old was able to answer them and seemed to enjoy this new adventure.

Jerry turned to me on the couch and said, "Why don't you go over to the Christian bookstore in town and get one of those books. I liked it and it wasn't so hard to do."

Wonder of wonders, it was all I could do to restrain the impulse to hug Jerry, hug the Moes, and do cartwheels in their formal living room. In a matter-of-fact voice, I smiled—with my heart in my throat—"Sure, I'll try to do that this week." (Try? I was their first customer on Monday morning!)

Our beginnings didn't go as smoothly as our free sample. Ours seemed formal, staged and unnatural. Yet when you think of it, worship is never a natural act for mortals. The angels do it effortlessly, but we have to work at it.

Jerry and I persisted. We endured short attention spans, little fingers that reached out during prayer time to pinch someone, wiggling, yawns, playing with cars and toys hidden in small pants pockets.

There were times when we said, "Do you think the children are getting **anything** out of this?" In spite of our doubts, we finished **Little Visits,** and went on to the next book, **More Little Visits.** After we completed that book, we went to the Christian bookstore for further suggestions.

I will tell you that there was never a time of easy victory for us when it came to the endurance test of holding nightly devotions. I'm sure I pushed harder than Jerry to keep them going, but it was truly a labor for love's sake.

Do you know how long it took before we felt comfortable and natural with this effort? Four years. By the time we had worked out the kinks, our youngest child was in kindergarten.

It is important to be aware that all spiritual endeavors take time. Don't be hard on yourselves and your loved ones for not catching on to things right away. Actually, you're "in process" the rest of your life, so don't worry. Relax.

When we started family devotions I immediately assumed Jerry and I would be able to pray together at night. But no. It was a couple of years before we prayed comfortably and openly with each other at bedtime. The darkness helped me get over my initial blushing, because I knew Jerry couldn't see me. Now I can pray in the middle of anything without blushing...holocaust, storm...anything.

I hope sharing these personal stories will be of help to you. It is naive to assume everything that works for me will work for you, but I hope you can walk away with some basic principles.

The next time you're on the phone and someone tells you of a problem, why not ask that individual, "How can I best pray for you this week?" That short phrase will force a complainer to focus on the main issue. It will also let a person you love know how far you will walk with him in his troubles. It just may open an unbeliever's mind to the awareness that God is in the business of answering prayers.

Does someone mock the idea of your praying? Tell him, "So humor me a little. Let's just see what happens, even if I'm the only one who believes in prayer." It may take a few such jolts to convince a person that God is really involved. Think of what an opportunity it is for God to establish His credibility!

Father, I'm nervous and scared and my heart beats so loudly when it comes to asking others to let me pray for them. Lead me to the place where I'll be able to risk my composure and self-image, if only to help You get closer to the ones I love. Amen.

CHAPTER 17

Pawnshop Prayer Box

There will be times in your life when God will want you to get your hands off something. It may be the thing that causes you to say, "My head hurts from bumping into this brick wall. I can't take it any more."

Getting your hands off something is easier said than done. You may say, "God I give up. You do the work in my loved one's life...I can't go any further," but it doesn't always help.

Or you may find yourself telling friends, "Yesterday, I gave this up to the Lord." A few days or weeks roll by and you've had your hands in the cookie jar again. So you say to your friends or your prayer group, "I thought I'd given it all up to the Lord, but I hadn't. Last night I **really** gave everything to the Lord."

Dare I say, this scenario might be repeated ad infinitum? The expression, "I gave it to the Lord," can become a glib phrase which is true only at the moment it is said.

When I'm in this sort of rut, I try to do something tangible. I physically separate myself from my prayer worry by writing it down on paper. I lay my hands on it, just like the Hebrew people did in the Old Testament when they offered their sacrifices. Sometimes I do this when I go to bed at night. I say, "God, I'm too sleepy to keep worrying about this all night. You do it for me." And then I take my hands off of it.

I've found another tangible plan that works for me.

Maybe it can help you if you have a tendency to repossess issues you've "really" left to the Lord. I call it my "Pawnshop Prayer Box."

Although I've never been in a pawnshop, I know that the customer brings an article in and leaves it with the pawnbroker in exchange for something he needs, usually money. In a spiritual sense, there comes a time when you must relinquish the physical holding of a worry, a time when you need to leave a prayer concern with a "heavenly" pawnbroker.

In exchange, God will give you the assurance that He is going to look after your anxiety. He tells you that you don't have to parade in front of the display window daily, and He asks you not to reclaim the worry by requesting it be removed from His safekeeping for you to handle again.

He knows you will be plagued by doubts. "It's been a week already and God hasn't answered my prayer. I wonder if He's forgotten. Maybe I should help God some way. There must be something I can do to get Him to answer earlier." He knows you're going to feel that way, so He gives you these words in Matthew 6:34:

"So don't be anxious about tomorrow. God will take care of your tomorrow too. Live one day at a time" (LB).

Knowing that verse doesn't make worry disappear, but for some, the physical act of letting go on paper helps put the verse into action.

I had read in a magazine about a technique that could accomplish this. After reading the article, I hurried to my basement to find the essential items to begin. Rummaging through my supply of assorted containers, I picked out two small jewelry-size cardboard boxes. On one I wrote, "Prayer requests I leave with God." On the other I wrote, "Prayers answered."

Then I began to try to put my requests into words. I thought I knew what I wanted, but I discovered my worries clouded my ability to think clearly. What did I really want God to do? Sometimes when I'd begin a sentence, I'd be struck by the idea, "This sounds silly. Why am I telling God how to answer this?"

My plan wasn't working so I had to re-think the prayer request idea. How could I phrase a request so that it wouldn't start with a complaint? I had to spend a few minutes thinking about asking for things my loved ones needed.

Instead of, "Lord, help this person to stop lying," I needed to say, "This person needs to value truth. Plant a desire for telling the truth."

Instead of saying, "Make _____(name)_____ stop being so inconsiderate," I reworded it to say, "Help _____(name)_____ to be concerned for the feelings of others. Let him hear himself as others hear him."

Seeing my prayer requests on paper in front of me gave me another faith boost. Once I could verbalize the requests, and clarify the needs of those for whom I was praying, much of my original worry lost its sting.

Not all the prayer requests were big items. I found the big items weren't the things that drained me of energy; the little things had the power to irritate like gnats. That first week I had six or seven prayer requests. Whenever I'd think of something that was draining me, I'd write it down and slip it into the box.

Whenever I put a slip in the box, I said this prayer (pasted on the inside of the lid): "Lord, I want to get my hands off this worry. It's dragging me down and depleting my reservoirs of strength. I desperately need You to carry this concern on my behalf, just like You promised You'd do when You died for me on Calvary."

Later that first week, I found a Bible verse that seemed appropriate. I typed it on a piece of paper and glued it to the front of the box. It read:

"Let him have all your worries and cares, for He is always thinking about you and watching everything that concerns you" (I Peter 5:7, LB).

After one month, I opened the "requests" box and transferred every answered prayer to the "answered" box. Over the next 12 months I was amazed to discover that at least 75% of my petitions had been taken care of without my worrying, and without my intervention. God had done things without me, and in many cases, quickly and effectively. It was a good thing I had stopped stirring the pot with my meddlesome spoon.

At the end of that year I learned something else about the value of the prayer boxes: **Whenever you're tempted to worry that God may forget you, you can look back and actually count the times He remembered!**

Did you know the Jews, God's chosen people, used to do that too? They didn't have cardboard boxes, but they had something else. Rocks. They used rocks to mark the places where God had intervened. The rocks became visible memorials to remind anyone who passed by. The practice also served to encourage the Israelites on dark days when they could have thought God had forgotten them.

Most of my life, I've found prayer to be an essential I can't live without. I've prayed for those who have lost their jobs, for lost articles, for those who have suffered disappointments. Even when God didn't answer as quickly as I'd hoped or in the way I had hoped, I was always sure He knew something I didn't. A seemingly unanswered prayer has never stopped me.

If you've ever been told by your loved one, "Keep out of my space...don't trespass on my life...mind your own business," perhaps this prayer box idea will help. During those times when we have no other recourse but prayer, we need visible assurances that we are in contact with Him.

CHAPTER 18

Do You Have A "10"?

On a scale of 1 to 10, with 10 being the most intense desire possible, where would you place your concern for a loved one? Before you answer "10" let me caution you. If you say "10," you're saying more than "I'm at the hand-wringing stage."

A 10 is more than a get-down-on-your-knees-and-pray-your-heart-out prayer. A 10 is a commitment. It means you are willing to deprive yourself of some comforts. A 10 is serious business.

Moses had a 10, and Jesus had a 10 in the Garden of Gethsemane. Daniel, Elijah and Noah each had a 10. What is your 10? For one person it might be the pain of watching a son or daughter give up the faith and turn to a life of open sin, to another an alcoholic spouse who needs healing in body and spirit, to another, a loved one who is dying and doesn't know Jesus.

Tens don't have to be events of earthshaking intensity. A 10 might be the inner feelings of inadequacy you feel when you are unable to reach out to help someone you love. When you've got a 10, you know it!

The Bible tells us of a tool powerful enough to change the course of history, and to change what is going on inside you. It is powerful enough to handle a 10. This tool is fasting.

The biblical kind of fasting will affect both you and your loved one **only** if it is accompanied by prayer. It's not some means by which you punish your body and go into public mourning; rather, it is a self-denial that says to God, "I'm here to do business!"

You'll quickly find out just how serious you really are. Every "tummy-rumbling" will remind you why you're on your knees, and a little hunger can suddenly seem important, unless you keep forcing your personal yearnings aside for the business at hand—the needs of your loved one.

The Bible talks of many different kinds of fasting. Bible heroes fasted on occasions of public disaster (1 Samuel 31:11-13), private affliction (1 Samuel 1:7), grief (2 Samuel 12:16), national repentance (1 Samuel 7:5,6), sad news (Nehemiah 1:4) and sacred ordination (Acts 13:3).

The key to fasting is to be sure it is what God wants you to do. It should be God's chosen fast. When you sense this as His choice of action for you, you'll see a difference in the outcome of prayers associated with fasting.

Why fast? By fasting, you eliminate the strain on your bodily functions (the strain caused by transferring foods into nutrients and the strain put on the various organs to process and assimilate those nutrients). You can concentrate better on rallying all your body's forces into the task of quality prayer. I would never have believed the difference in prayer power until I tried fasting. It felt like a "hot-line" to heaven.

However, fasting is not to be used to manipulate God into getting what you want from Him. Instead, it is to help you focus on how God must feel as He watches your loved one. When you absorb God's ache as your own, then you have a sense of what it means to pray "according to His will."

Beginners are encouraged to start with a fasting period that eliminates just one meal. That was a considerable comfort for me, because in my first thoughts of fasting I imagined myself in a dungeon starving to death for some worthy cause. Beginners can sit quietly, read a few passages in the Bible, stop and pray, sing, listen to Christian music. There is much that can be done.

Arthur Wallis, in his book, **God's Chosen Fast,** explains fasting much better than I can. He points out the difference between the 40-day fasts of Jesus and Moses and shorter fasting periods. I was surprised to learn that fasting practices may vary considerably. Some practices eliminate both food and drink while others maintain liquids during the fast period. I usually keep up a fluid intake of fruit juices or bouillon during fasting, since I otherwise get dizzy and feel faint.

Some of my most beautiful moments alone with God have been during times of fasting. I encourage you to look to your heart and the yearnings for your loved ones. Is it possible God is calling you to a fasting period for someone?

If you have been avoiding deep intercessory prayer, God may allow things to become much worse so you'll recognize it's time to get serious. You see, not only does your loved one possibly need to "hit bottom" to recognize his spiritual need, but you may have to hit a low point as well, in order to have the measure of prayer commitment God wants.

CHAPTER 19

How Can I Know
If I'm The One To Witness?

How can you know? Two questions can help you find out. First, are any of your witnessing attempts making headway? Second, do witnessing situations crop up naturally?

If both answers are yes, that's an indication you are strategically in good position for God to use you.

Even if you can't answer the above questions with a yes, that doesn't eliminate you from the picture. However, it may mean you aren't the one God wants to use in a primary role.

I usually suggest a person ask some soul-searching questions about this matter. For instance, "Am I forcing a witnessing situation because I assume I'm the only one who cares enough to get the job done?"

Another question to help you determine your effectiveness would be, "Am I too close to a loved one physically or emotionally?" Even doctors don't operate on members of their immediate family. They know their judgment may be clouded by emotion during a crisis.

How about you? Do you rush in like the proverbial bull in the china shop? Are you too close emotionally to your loved ones to function in a rational manner when you're under pressure?

Is it possible that your witnessing style and the personality needs of your loved one are not compatible? Refer again to the earlier chapter which shows the personality types and the scrimmage line that separates them.

The next thing I do is pray for insight to know if this job "has my name on it." My mind and my heart might be shouting "yes" but my spirit might be directing, "Halt...this one's not yours."

I find a time when I know I won't be interrupted. I ask the questions below and wait a minute or so in between each. (That way God can get a word in, if He wants to!)

1. Would you show me if I'm forcing a witnessing situation?

2. Am I too close to be used?

3. Am I getting in the way?

4. Should I pray for another to be called to witness in my place?

How would you go about praying in regard to that last question? I suggest you get on your knees and say, "Lord, if not me—then who?" and just sit quietly before God. Does someone's name occur to you? A face flash in your mind? Don't discount it. Jot it down. Are there other names? Sometimes your subconscious will project a "logical" choice, but you still need the test of time to determine God's choice.

You might want to pray for the persons whose names come to mind. Ask God to put a hunger in their heart if they are the ones He has chosen. Then pray that God will anoint the witnessing time, if and when it comes.

The next day, pray over the list again. Any new names? You may feel strongly that God might be able to use one of those persons, but **resist the urge to tell them right away.** Don't rush to the phone and say, "Guess what? God has just told me you are the one." While that may be true, you shouldn't say it. In your sense of urgency, you may place an unwarranted burden on another. **Pressure should come from God, not you.**

What, then, can you do? I suggest you casually say to your possible-messenger-to-be that you're concerned

about your loved one. Tell of a few particulars and, if possible, put into words what your loved one needs most. Then you could say, "If God lays it upon your heart to add _____ to your prayer list, fine. I'm trusting God has the answers."

In that way, if God does the urging, you will not have to implore and furthermore, you won't have to be disappointed if the would-be-messenger doesn't follow through.

You may think that is an overly casual attitude especially if you feel it is a life and death matter. A number of times over the years, I've awakened in the middle of the night and have been strongly impressed to pray for a friend, a member of the family, an acquaintance or even a television personality. I didn't think up those times—God did. Having had that happen to me, it has been a comfort to know that whenever God needs to awaken a prayer warrior, He can do it. God can call anybody at any time—awake or asleep. (Let God be God; that's what He does best).

In my earliest years of trying to share my faith with others, I thought every "prayer bundle" had my name on it. I'd get an idea, prepare myself with prayer, stick a few tracts in my purse and dash off to someone's house. The "someone" could have been a person I thought was heading in the wrong direction, one who had had an argument with another Christian brother or sister, someone in depression, etc.

Sometimes I was the right person for them. Often I was the wrong one and I shook my head in bewilderment. How could I be the wrong person? I had prayed, hadn't I? I was so sure God had nudged me to visit them. Sometimes they would be leaving for an appointment, sometimes they were not even at home. So why did I feel led to go?

I think God was testing my obedience. Was I willing to go if He called?

A number of years ago I flew to Michigan to visit my mother who was recovering from a staph infection in her hip. Something told me I needed to speak to Mother about spiritual things. I had a gnawing feeling she was wrestling with some problem. Although she had gone to church for years, we had never had deep discussions on spiritual growth and maturity.

A few days before going, I had borrowed a book called **Evangelism Explosion,** written by Dr. James Kennedy of Coral Ridge Presbyterian Church in Ft. Lauderdale, Florida. It was a step-by-step procedure developed to help laymen in sharing their faith with others.

Glancing through the materials, I had regretted not having had the time to digest the course outline. In many ways, it was as though I had read a manual on how to perform brain surgery, and then was expected to perform all the steps from memory! Had I studied the course, I'd have had those steps memorized and I'd have been conditioned in advance. But I was definitely not prepared. Oh well, I thought, it's better than nothing.

I was home for just a few days, and it wasn't until the last day of my stay that Mother and I were finally alone.

I had just begun to open a discussion about spiritual concerns when the nurse came in.

"Sorry, you'll have to step outside. The doctor wants to examine Mrs. Kurtz," she said.

I followed her instructions and then re-entered the room. I began again, and another nurse came in.

"I'm sorry, you'll have to leave again. It's time to change her bandages."

By the time they had finished, I looked at the clock. Visiting hours were over. It wouldn't be long before I'd have to catch my flight back to Boston.

"Well, Lord," I said, "I guess I was not ready. At least You know I was willing. Maybe another time?"

I continued to think of the "aborted mission" as I drove home from the airport. My mind was obsessed with the idea of finding another who could go in my place. Who might it be?

Driving along, I began to think of the possibilities. Why not write a letter to the chaplain at the hospital?

The thought remained on my mind for several days. Finally, I pulled out my stationery and proceeded to write to the chaplain. I encouraged him to call on my mother. Later he wrote me a cordial reply indicating he would continue to drop in on her from time to time, but I was still in a state of unrest.

While praying about the matter, a woman's name popped into my mind, Mabel Matthews. I hadn't thought of her in years. I remembered she and my mother used to play bridge together 10 or 12 years earlier.

Why not ask Mabel to pray for Mother? Hmmm, I wondered, has God put her name in my mind? I would soon find out.

A few days after mailing a letter to Mabel, I received this reply.

"Dear Nyla,

"I dropped everything the moment I received your letter. Your mother has been on my mind for some time and your letter served to activate my good intentions.

"You said you were concerned about your mother's salvation. I should tell you that my husband and I have been attending a training program for the past three years. It's called the Evangelism Explosion. I asked your mother the two questions we have found helpful in addressing the salvation question.

"First, 'Have you come to the place in your spiritual life where you can say you know for certain that if you were to die today, you would go to heaven?' The second question is, 'Suppose you were to die today and stand before God, and He were to say to you, "Why should I let you into My heaven" what would you say?'

"Your mother said, 'Well, I've tried to live a good life and be kind to others.'

"To much of the world, those answers sound humble and nice. But they aren't the answers God has given us in the Bible.

"We can know for certain, the Bible says, without a doubt, that the promise of heaven is ours.

"I plan to stick by your mother and visit her at regular

intervals until she can answer those questions with certainty.

Lovingly,
Mabel"

I wept when I read the letter. That was the same program and book I had tried to cram-study before I went to see Mother!

Mabel did continue to visit my mother. She gave Mother a modern translation of the Bible and showed her how to find assurance passages in Scripture.

A few weeks later I received another note from Mabel.

"I think your mother knows the way to heaven. She has her assurance. Virginia knows that nothing she could ever do would be good enough to gain her entry into heaven. It's **only** because of the free gift of eternal life offered by Jesus to those who accept it."

I literally danced around the house, clutching the letter and shouting, "Thank You, Jesus; Thank You, Lord. You did it; **You** did it!"

Even though we may be physically absent, God still can do great things! Sometimes He can perform even greater things because we're not there. (Not always, but it is good to know it is possible.)

I suspect I'm not all that effective in witnessing to members of my immediate family, anyway. Most Christians find this to be true. Even Jesus had the same problem. Those who rubbed elbows with Him daily often had the greatest difficulty accepting His divinity, especially the people who lived in the town of Nazareth. They all took Him for granted. It is odd to think we would believe strangers, or somebody we see on television, more than someone we live with.

So what can you do when you determine you are the one God has chosen? Here are some suggestions. Keep channels of communication open, even if it means biting your tongue at times. Don't disagree with loved ones at every objectionable comment. A judicious guarding of your tongue can mean the difference in being truly "heard" and being considered as nothing more than a clanging bell.

If doors open easily for sharing, fine. Otherwise, wait. Don't instigate fights or scrimmages.

Save "Christianese" and other fancy "God words" for those who understand what they mean, or who really want to know what it means to be "sanctified," "justified," and "saved." Ask God to help you think of everyday examples that don't involve those words.

Ask God to help you in your maturity. Trust that you won't always feel inadequate in sharing your faith. Take a course in witnessing.

Above all, when you know you're definitely not the one God is planning to use, put your arms around your prayers. Be tenacious. Be persistent. Never give up!

If Abraham had to wait for 50 years before he saw God fulfill an earlier promise of a son...if Sarah could wait beyond the childbearing years, then you can know that no matter how impossible the situation, nothing is too hard for God.

When you are wrestling with the unseen forces that vie for men's souls, you have to dream impossible dreams. When you go into battle to win others to Christ, you have to put on more than just your helmet of salvation. You have to use all the armor God provides; you have to be strong in the Lord (Ephesians 6:10).

Why? Because you're fighting Satan. Even if you've always believed Satan is a myth, that's not what the Bible says. "For we wrestle not against flesh and blood, but against principalities, against powers, against the rulers of the darkness of this world, against spiritual wickedness in high places" (Ephesians 6:12, KJV).

———————

All right, so I'm not a dynamo as an evangelist and my 38-year-old vocal chords crack when I sing soprano. If God gives me something I can do well, I ought to do it. The same should be true for you. And that's why I press this message on you... **so maybe you aren't called to be the one to witness. Pray. In the long run that may be a far more potent weapon in your hands than anything you've tried.**

To illustrate my point, let me tell you about my brother. Mark had been searching for a personal relationship with Christ for many years. It was a quiet search. He had always found it difficult to believe that

Jesus died for the sins of the world, and that He also died for Mark.

I had watched Mark struggle as he moved from one loyalty to another, never quite sure what he wanted. Mark was always certain that something "way out there" would be the gold at the end of the rainbow.

We occasionally talked through the years about goals and direction. I always found a way to remind Mark that God was his source of direction. But Mark and I do not have the luxury of proximity; we live thousands of miles apart. A brief conversation or two scattered over telephone wires at holiday times has never been my idea of the best kind of witnessing.

Were we to live closer, perhaps my references to God in conversation would be no more effective than they have been. One thing I know—being separated by distance has caused my prayer life to grow stronger.

I remember one Christmas when Jerry and I had taken the children and gone home to Michigan for the holidays. Mark and I went shopping together, and in our moments alone, he confessed that as much as he wanted God in his life, he just couldn't cross over the line. Something always stopped him.

I tried to comfort him, but I could see my words weren't making any sense. Mark couldn't grasp what I was saying—not because he wasn't bright, but because he didn't have the Holy Spirit's illumination.

I recalled feeling helpless at the end of our conversation. All I could do was reach over and give Mark a big hug.

I went home with a burden in my heart. Continuing to pray for Mark, I asked the Lord to lead someone else into his life who could help him understand. Over the years I would hear of Christian roommates who had been assigned to Mark. I'd pray again, "Thank you, God." But for six years nothing happened.

Then one day I received a call. Mark's first words were, "Guess what, Sis. It finally happened."

I didn't even know what he was talking about. "What do you mean?" I asked.

He kept me in suspense, making me guess. I guessed everything.

Finally he said, "It's something I bet you've been praying about."

Then I understood. Mark had finally found Jesus. He told me it had happened at work the night before. A temporary-help man had been assigned to his supervisory area. During the few days this man worked under Mark he casually shared his faith with him. That night, he had pointed his finger at Mark and said, "This is **your** time...and we both know it."

Jim Daniels was the man of God's choosing that night. He opened his Bible, which he kept at work, and showed Mark the right passages. Mark broke down and wept. Finally, Mark had recognized Jesus' desire for him. It didn't matter who knew it...Mark couldn't hide the tears of cleansing. He let the "waters" flow in front of Jim, God and everybody.

———————

Do you have loved ones who are saved, but who balk at the prospects of learning how to live an abundant life after conversion? (Many believers suffer from "arrested development." If that is the case, your prayer warrior days are still ahead of you.) They can't understand that it is important to go on with Christ and you scratch your head, wondering why they don't grow. The more impatient you become, the more difficult it is to nudge and encourage without sounding pushy. That person may be saying to himself, "Wow, I am saved and still she's not satisfied."

Here is an analogy you might find helpful if the Lord ever opens the doors for future sharing on the subject.

Suppose you bought a new wonder gadget and brought it home from the store. You open the box, remove the contents and casually set the instructions aside. In time, you totally misplace the instructions and you find that you can remember how to use the gadget only for a few simple functions.

Still more time passes and because you do not use this wonder gadget for the 30 or 40 operations advertised, you tend to let it gather dust on your shelf. Eventually, you stop using it altogether and, in fact, you go back to your earlier methods of performing various jobs. You walk by your shelf and look up longingly, "Yes, I sure wanted that gadget badly in the beginning. Maybe if I'd used it more..."

Your faith is the same way. No one will take your salvation from you. But if you don't consult the "manufacturer's handbook" (the Bible), you will fail to see how essential and practical salvation is for every facet of your life.

In time, unless you maintain fellowship with other "users," you may decide to return to the pre-salvation methods for solving your problems. You're back where you started, left holding the item that has printed on its side: "Good only when used. Satisfaction guaranteed only if plugged into the divine source of energy."

That analogy came to me because of a dear Christian woman who has been slacking off in her "practicing" of the faith. I love her very much and I ache to encourage her without pushing. (Is it possible God places in our paths others whose baby steps falter, just so that we will learn to explain our faith better? If we don't have someone who makes us ache, we don't learn as much.)

———————

Father, I don't always recognize the "bundles" with my name on them. Help me stop and read labels more carefully so I won't pick up the wrong packages. Amen.

Section Five

PROFITING FROM YOUR MISTAKES

From Mistake to Miracle

Forgive, Even If You Can't Forget

CHAPTER 20

From Mistake To Miracle

I can't guarantee that if you eliminate all the mistakes and manipulative techniques in your witnessing you'll suddenly see your loved ones come to the Lord. But I do believe you'll be more likely to experience a far greater strengthening of your own relationship with God.

You know what the Bible says about getting the log out of your own eye before you meddle with the splinter in another's. It makes sense. You need to concentrate on yourself without becoming selfish and introverted about your faith.

And yet, in spite of your mistakes and mine, we hear stories of people who develop a relationship with God in the unlikeliest of situations.

God may choose at any time to take blatant mistakes and turn them around. That doesn't give us the license to continue to put roadblocks in the pathway of potential believers. We must eliminate barriers wherever we can. We should remember God is going to be sovereign and do what He wants, with whom He wants, when He wants.

Ultimately God is still God. He's going to do what He does best. We're not in charge—He is.

So you may find yourself full to the eyebrows with spiritual advice for those around you. You may be like the man who became a Christian, and decided his family was going to have devotions and prayers in the morning at breakfast, whether they liked it or not! This man, with an authoritarian hand, passed an edict and was committed to making it stick.

His wife, in shock, began to balk and rebel against this husband whom she thought had become a fanatic. So upset was she that when she happened to turn on television one day and overheard a Christian talk-show host mention a phone number to call, she called in to complain about the "madman" she was living with. She wanted to give the Christians on the other end of the line a piece of her mind.

After she'd gone on for some time with her list of complaints, the person on the other end of the line said, "Tell me, do you know what commitment your husband was making when he decided to become a Christian?"

No, she wasn't certain. All she could see was that her life had been disrupted.

"May I explain it to you?" the voice inquired, and ten minutes later this resistant wife found herself asking the telephone counselor to help her receive Jesus too.

Yes, it does happen. And do you know why? It's because God sees you as a "seed planter." Some of us will be master planters, He knows. Others, He sees, will make mistakes but we will be sincere. Some He will bless with the ability to water the seeds as well as plant them. But He reserves the right to be the force that makes things grow.

When I first discovered that the Holy Spirit is the one who will "close the sale" and make the conversion happen, it set me free. It helped me forgive myself and stop feeling guilty over past failures and indiscretions.

Lord, when You want an appointment with our loved one, when it's on Your calendar of "things to do today," Your sovereignty won't let anything stop You. And furthermore, we realize that if our loved one gets right with You, we still can't take credit for it. It's still Your miracle. Thank You, Lord. Amen.

CHAPTER 21

Forgive, Even If You Can't Forget

The biggest hurdle, in my mind, in reaching loved ones is forgiving them for not accepting our message, forgiving ourselves for not being able to win them to Christ, and forgiving God for not reaching them when we wanted it to happen "yesterday."

God must have known that unforgiveness is like a cancer in a believer's life. That's why He included the implied admonition in His model prayer to forgive your brother his trespasses (sins) just as God forgives you of yours. The fact is, when you forgive, God can forgive you too.

I've known Christians who were so bitter they couldn't say the words, "I forgive." I've known people who, in spite of hearing sermons on forgiveness and reconciliation, have continued to hold grudges. In those cases, even fellow believers proved unable to change the animosity. No Bible verses helped, no prayers altered events. And the enmity continued to fester.

Bitterness is never a pretty picture. Eventually it shows up in the mirror with lines around the eyes and mouth and a permanent scowl. Not an attractive picture and certainly not an image that would draw anyone to Christ.

Others who observe this in a Christian feel justified in saying, "Her God is a powerless God." Or, "Why should I believe what he says about God; it hasn't made any difference in his life."

I realize some of you are deeply hurt by wrongs done to you by your loved ones. You haven't been able to forgive, even though you wish you could.

Maybe that certain incident when someone shamed you or embarrassed you or physically abused you is still too vivid in your mind. You can't let it loose.

I don't claim to have easy answers, even though my writing style might lead you to believe otherwise. I've wrestled like you have and I confess to having entertained unforgiveness for years, the kind that makes one replay the home movies of memories over and over.

A forced "I'm sorry" or "I forgive you" comes out as if some parent has just marched us in front of our adversary and compelled us to curtsy and say mechanically, "I forgive." Frankly, too often the heart hasn't forgiven when the mouth has.

Some of us can forgive certain offenses, provided they don't include gossip about our family members, remarks about our pets, insults about our intelligence, slurs against our religious or political persuasions. There seems to be a place in our minds that holds file folders labeled "unforgivables."

I think we are wrong when we try to play judge. We snatch judgeship from God's hands, especially if it seems to us He's not doing His job by visibly punishing wrongdoing before our eyes.

Suppose you can't say, "I forgive." Could you, instead, be willing to say to God, "I'm willing to be made willing to forgive"? Most of us can at least warm up to that one.

It's hard to say, "Move over, hate, make room for love." But sometimes we have to talk to ourselves and hear ourselves say out loud, "I can't forgive _____(name)_____ yet, but I'm willing to be made willing." When you can say that, you're at least half-way ready and there's hope for you.

The next thing you might do is say to yourself, "This thing is too big for me. I think I'll work up my forgiving skills by practicing on something smaller."

Make a list of some of the things you could forgive, like an unmade bed, tools left lying on the garage floor, shirts that were laid out to be mended (but a certain "somebody" never got to them!), a letter a secretary forgot to mail.

Then practice the art of "sundowning." Sundowning means you don't let the anger persist after the sun sets. (That comes from Ephesians 4:26.)

Let's apply that principle. Suppose you and your spouse (or roommate) have had an argument. Each one thinks he is right.

Rule number one: **Never solve a problem while you're still smoldering.** Back off for a cooling down.

Rule number two: **Write down your grievance on paper so you can see it and get a handle on it.** Some things will strike you as absurd once you see them in black and white. Other times you'll see your thoughts so clearly you'll be better armed for a new discussion.

Rule number three: **Don't give that note or hate slip to anybody.** (Guideline: if the note isn't something that builds or uplifts, it's not worth sharing.)

Rule number four: **Write an uplifting note**—one that says something like: "I can't handle my feelings when I get upset with you. I can't say you're right about the matter we were discussing, but I know I need to forgive both you and myself for allowing this thing to get out of hand. I want to go to bed with a clean slate. I don't mean that the problem must be solved; I only want to retain the idea that we can work things out eventually."

See if the above example lines up with the following Scripture: "Finally, all of you, have unity of spirit, sympathy, love of the brethren, a tender heart and a humble mind. Do not return evil for evil or reviling for reviling, but on the contrary, bless, for to this you have been called that you may obtain a blessing (I Peter 3:8,9, RSV).

So your roommate doesn't understand your faith and is threatening to move out. So your children rebel at your desire to nurture them in the admonition of the Lord. So your associates at work criticize you publicly. Yes, you're going to experience some strong feelings of anger and resentment. You wouldn't be normal if you didn't. God never said, "Thou shalt not be angry," but He did say, "Never let the sun go down on your anger." He also said, "Be angry and sin not" (Ephesians 4:26).

There's another Bible verse that has helped me through those times. Maybe it will help you too:

"No temptation (fill in the word that describes the anger you feel) has overtaken you that is not common to man. God is faithful, and he will not let you be tempted beyond your strength, but with the temptation will also provide the way of escape, that you may be able to endure it" (I Corinthians 10:13, RSV).

Could forgiveness be that way of endurance?

When I was a little girl I lived with anger. Whenever my father spoke crossly to me, which happened often, I harbored a grudge. I can remember sitting in the back seat of the car after being reprimanded for starting a fight with my brother.

I always thought I was innocent, but I guess that's the way all kids think. So I'd sit and sulk and promise myself, "I'll fix him." How hard I tried to keep my promise, a promise that lasted at best for 15 minutes. Then I would be angry at myself for failing to follow through with my intentions.

All those grudges piled on top of each other make a very tall wall. I lived behind that wall for 35 years before I decided to do something about it.

One day my friend Sonja and I had a discussion about Christians being poor at accepting gifts. A thought struck me, "I wonder if I have trouble accepting God's gifts because I've never been able to accept gifts from other people?"

After Sonja left, I brooded over that thought. Was there a connection between my spiritual difficulties and my unforgiveness? Just as I fought accepting gifts from my earthly father, was I now fighting the gifts God wanted to offer me? Was there a parallel?

For days the same thoughts kept coming back. I didn't realize this was God's way of wearing down my resistance and making me receptive to His next project for me. I had to find out if unforgiveness was at the core. So I decided to write a letter of apology—not for being wrong, per se, but for being wrong in holding a grudge all those years:

"Dear Dad,

"I've come to the place where I can't go any further until I get something from you. Remember when I was little and you used to reprimand me? Right now I can't think of any specific situation in detail, so I don't know if I was right or wrong or even justified in my anger. This I do know...the resentment is getting in the way of my spiritual growth and I can't go on until I'm freed of it.

Love,

Nyla Jane"

A few days later, I received his reply:

"My Dear,

"For whatever forgiveness you feel you need, you have it from me. I wouldn't want to do anything to stand in the way of your spiritual growth.

Love,

Dad"

Oh, how I cried as I clutched that letter. Free at last! I didn't know it would feel so good.

That was the beginning of some important breakthroughs in my life. Not only did I experience a healing of memories, but certain physical ailments either improved or left completely. I wondered if Dad would receive anything from this.

I received a call from him a few months later. We had never discussed spiritual experiences or divine intervention, but on this occasion Dad didn't need to say "divine intervention," because we both knew that was what had happened.

Dad called to tell me of this unusual experience. He tried to phone a lawyer to start some legal proceedings based on a grudge against someone, but he did not reach the number intended. "I thought I dialed the correct number," he said, "but a voice on the other end said, 'This is a recording. You have just reached Dial-A-Prayer'.

"After the minister concluded his recorded message, his last words were, 'There's something you are about to do that is wrong. Don't do it'. Nyla, I think God helped me; I think He did."

I thought of all the years I wrote funny notes to remind him to start going back to church. Dad had always been a "late bloomer" in spiritual matters, waiting until he was in his thirties before he really started his Christian life. He'd gotten sidetracked and pulled away because he couldn't forgive the inconsistencies and lack of perfection in Christians. (Eventually he again began to give God his verbal allegiance but he couldn't bring himself to resume a relationship with a church.)

Once I sent Dad a tract just to jog his memory. Knowing he spent his Sundays communing with God in nature, I wrote on the inside cover, "This is for the next time you're in 'church' on the Au Sable River."

It was only after his death that I found out the depth of his spiritual life after he left church. I discovered there had been special times with Mother when he prayed for her, and he had had a friend with whom he prayed on his knees.

After death, I realize there is a tendency to venerate departed loved ones, to make them "saintly" and overlook their flaws. I don't want my comments about my father to be taken as exoneration. He may have been a prodigal in many ways, but that is not for me to judge. That's God's job. I would like to believe, however, that

Bill Kurtz was a forgiven prodigal, by God's grace. And I thank God that I had my chance to experience the healing which comes with forgiveness—before my father died.

Maybe you'll never experience the assurance that your loved ones have been forgiven by God. But you can experience forgiveness yourself as you release previous judgments and let bitterness die. Give God the chance to heal you before it's too late.

Can you say with your lips, "Lord I forgive ___(name)___ for being himself"? "I forgive ___(name)___ for being herself"? "Forgive **me** for being myself"?

I prayed God would give me an ending that would usher in the beginning of a new life for you. A chapter on forgiveness seemed a strange ending for new beginnings, and yet that sums it up. That's the secret in "letting go and letting God." Without forgiveness, you can't let go.

Your forgiveness sets God free to work dynamically in the lives of those who are fighting Him.

When I started forgiving, I stopped pushing so hard. It released Jerry to be God's man, in God's way. Oh, he's still a conservative, keep-it-simple Christian. That's a good balance for me. I'm the balloon in the family and he's the ballast that keeps me stationary; he's the guidewires that keep me from drifting. Neither of us has changed a lot in basic temperament, but we've been changed in many other ways.

I watched Jerry grow from a man who used to say, "I'll never be able to get Christianity to apply to my business life," into a man who stopped praying only for himself and started praying for the people who work for him and those whose names appear daily on his appointment calendar. The more he has prayed for them, the more God has blessed: personally, spiritually, financially, professionally—in every way.

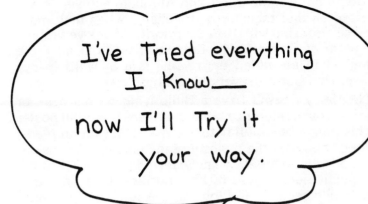

God did the same thing with Abraham and Jacob and blessed all that their hands touched...when they made their relationship with Him top priority. "Seek ye first the kingdom of God and His righteousness, and all these things shall be added unto you," is a by-word in our house. That sums up everything, doesn't it?

No, Jerry doesn't have a Bible lying on his desk or tracts on the conference table. But there is a small poster on his wall, a beautiful nature scene. The caption reads, "When I consider the majesty of the universe, I consider the God who made it." I know Jerry is not afraid to tell prospective employees of his priorities: God first, wife and family second, and job third. And I can remember when the order of those priorities was reversed.

I tiptoed past the living room the other day because I happened to see a man kneeling beside the sofa. He was holding a card in his hand, and I knew he was praying for the day's appointments and the problems of the men and women who were coming to see him.

I prayed, "Thank you, Lord, for Jerry, and for the fact that I finally learned to sit back, cease from meddling, and concentrate on my own shortcomings instead of his.

"Thank you, Lord, for Jerry, **just as he is.**"

Addendum

Two years after the "household plants" and other ploys ceased, Jerry Witmore was selected to be the focus of a newspaper editorial entitled, "Born-Again Christian Businessman" (**Wall Street Journal,** Oct. 24, 1977).

For Your Information

Books on Witnessing and Attitudes

Bright, Bill, "Have You Heard of the Four Spiritual Laws?" 1965, Campus Crusade for Christ, Inc. (A handy pocket-size tract that visually helps you explain salvation to another.)

Bright, Bill, "Have You Made the Wonderful Discovery of the Spirit-Filled Life?" 1966, Campus Crusade for Christ, Inc. (Helps a believer explain, in tract form, the means for moving beyond salvation to the abundant life Christ promises.)

Christenson, Evelyn, **Lord Change Me!** 1977, Victor Books (Scripture Press). (A book to help the believer concentrate on the beam that is in one's own eye.)

Jacksmann, Allan Hard, and Martin, Simon P., **Little Visits With God,** (also **More Little Visits With God**) Concordia Publishers, 1957. (This is an excellent book for sharing your faith with young families.)

Kennedy, James, **Evangelism Explosion,** 1970, Tyndale House. (Excellent overview with dialogue for explaining the basics of the Christian faith. Excellent training manual. Training program also available in many churches.)

Handford, Elizabeth Rice, **Me? Obey Him?** 1972, Sword Of The Lord Publishers, Murfreesboro, Tennessee. (While you may not agree with some of the con-

cepts, there is considerable food for thought for the
overzealous wife.)

Books on Prayer and Fasting

Wallis, Arthur, **God's Chosen Fast,** 1970, Christian Light
Publishers, Box 1126 Harrisonburg, Va. 22801

Books on Prayer

Two books I've found unusually helpful are...

Christenson, Evelyn, **What Happens When Women Pray,**
1975, Victor Books (Scripture Press)

Rinker, Rosalind, **Prayer, Conversing With God,** 1959,
Zondervan